Collins *gem*

Trees

Alastair Fitter
Illustrations by David More

HarperCollins*Publishers*

77-85 Fulham Palace Road
London W6 8JB
www.collins.co.uk

First published 1980
This edition published 2004

08

9 8 7 6

ISBN - 13: 978 0 00 718306 7

Design by Liz Bourne
Printed in China by Leo Paper Products

Find out more about HarperCollins and the environment at
www.harpercollins.co.uk/green

Contents

4

Introduction

TREES AND HOW THEY GROW

'Tree' is one of those useful words that have no precise definition, yet are immediately understood. Most botanists envisage a plant more than 3–4m high, with a single woody stem that persists for many years, and a branched crown. The extremes are clear-cut – a well-grown beech or pine is indubitably a tree – but there is a grey area between 'trees' and 'shrubs'. Apple trees for example frequently branch at ground level, but can still produce a crown 8–10m high, whereas blackthorn is almost always a shrub, forming a dense tangled mass with no stems, but if drawn up by the shade cast by surrounding trees, it produces a single trunk and a respectable small tree.

The word tree, therefore, best describes a form of growth rather than an individual species, so this book includes species such as osier, blackthorn and alder buckthorn that are normally shrubs, but which do grow into small trees occasionally.

How, then, does a plant turn into a tree? First it must lay down wood: this is produced when xylem, the tissue in plant stems which transports water from roots to leaves, becomes thick-walled and toughened. Secondly, the stem must stay alive for many seasons, which means that the buds must be borne on the tip of the shoot and not at ground level, as in tall herbaceous plants, in order to survive cold winters or other extreme conditions.

Of course the main advantage of being a tree is to be tall and so to get more light than surrounding plants. But basic engineering constraints require the strengthening of the base of the stem that provides support. This is brought about partly by the growth of the root system, anchoring the whole plant, and partly by the gradual thickening of the stem. Each year the whole stem from top to bottom puts on a new outer layer, so that the trunk becomes gradually thicker towards the base, and the resultant shape is in fact almost perfect from an engineer's standpoint. If you measure the height and girth of several specimens of a single species of tree you will find that there is a very close relationship maintained between them, almost throughout its life.

This continuous outward growth means that the conducting tissues are always on the edge of a tree trunk (which is why you can kill a tree by ring-barking it), and the older tissues in the centre of the trunk serve as tough

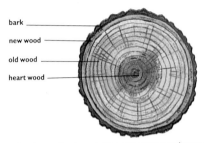

bark

new wood

old wood

heart wood

supporting tissues, the channels that once transported water to the leaves eventually being filled in. In temperate regions, with a cold winter during which growth ceases, this form of growth produces annual rings, which can be used to date a felled tree.

SOME PROBLEMS OF BEING A TREE

Most trees, except when planted for ornament, grow in woods and not as isolated specimens. Those magnificent trees that adorn the parks of stately homes are rather exceptional in the tree world. Few of their relations will get the chance to expand in all directions without coming up against neighbours. So, while the parkland tree grows up and out, its woodland counterpart is drawn always upward, for a tree that failed to do so would soon be overshadowed by those around it.

The shapes of trees, then, reflect their way of life. But living in woods imposes other constraints, for survival and success for a species involves shedding good seed that grows into new trees. When a seed germinates on the floor of a wood, it has little chance of growing steadily to the canopy 20, 30, perhaps even 50 metres above it. There is too little light to allow that. Instead the seedling must wait for a tree to fall or die, letting in light, and so allowing the race for the tree-tops to begin. In a beechwood you will see many young trees a few centimetres high, but very few more than that, except where a tree has fallen some years before. There, the gap will be filled with a mass of young trees, often ash or

sycamore, growing into the space. Underneath them, growing more slowly, but more tolerant of the shade they cast, will be the young beech trees, one of which will eventually become the new occupant of that particular patch of sunlight.

WHAT TO DO IN WINTER?

All plants in temperate regions have to survive winter.
Annuals simply disappear and survive as seeds; herbaceous
perennials keep their buds near or in the ground, where they
can be better protected. But a tree must have its buds high
up, where the battle for light is taking place. This is why
deciduous trees lose their leaves each autumn, leaving the
frost-resistant buds on the high branches, to grow a new
crop of leaves each spring. Deciduousness does involve an
enormous waste of resources – all those dead leaves – but it
means that the leaves themselves need not be frost-resistant
and so can be much more efficient. In arctic regions the
forests are of evergreen trees whose leaves need to be frost
resistant. This makes them less efficient but enables them to
survive all year round.

WHY BE A TREE?

The chief advantage in being a tree is the amount of light it
gets simply by being bigger than other plants. The
disadvantage of being a tree is that it must survive in one
place for a long time. If fires, landslides, or hurricanes are
regular events, the tree may die without ever having
reproduced. In fact in most temperate regions the natural
environment does favour trees in most places, and human
activity is the major factor militating against them. For
example it is thought that in about 4000 BC almost the
whole of Britain was covered by woodland, and it has mostly
been cleared by people using axes or fire.

WOODLANDS

Some trees grow faster than others. The typical forest trees,
such as oak and beech, are rather slow-growing compared to
such trees as birch and alder. These can almost be thought of
as tree 'weeds', for they have a surprising amount in common
with garden weeds. They produce huge numbers of very small
seeds, sometimes with wings, which travel considerable
distances, and are likely to fall in a place where no trees are
growing. Once there they grow rapidly and begin to produce
new seeds when perhaps as little as five years old, to start the
cycle off again.

In contrast oak trees produce many fewer seeds, but their
acorns contain lots of food for the developing seedling, giving
it a good start in life, particularly if it finds itself under a
canopy of other trees. On the other hand an acorn is not
well adapted to travelling long distances unless a jay or a
squirrel carries it off and buries it. Once established the
seedling grows rather slowly and may not produce seed until
it is 20 or 30 years old.

Woods tend, therefore, to be composed of these longer-
lived trees, of which the best example is oak. Over most of
Britain and much of Europe the vegetation that would occur
in the absence of human interference is oakwood of some
sort, although several different species of oak are involved. In
Britain the other important forest-forming trees are beech,
which grows best on the dry chalk hills and sands of southern
England; Scots pine which once formed extensive forests in
Scotland; ash which is characteristic of steep limestone valleys
in northern and western England; and alder which grows in
wet valleys and fens.

Birch is also now a common woodland tree, but it owes its prominence to man, for it is normally a coloniser of areas that have been cleared and then abandoned, such as heaths and moors.

There are of course many other trees, each with its own niche, but few of them really form woods. Some are common in woods, usually as rather isolated individuals, while others are introduced and are found either in plantations or in parks and gardens.

PEOPLE AND WOODLANDS

In Britain there are a few areas that have been woodland throughout all or most of their history – survivors of the ancient forests that once covered the country. They have a richer flora and fauna and, in particular, more of the unusual trees and shrubs (such as wild service tree) than the more recent plantations.

To our ancestors the wood was an essential part of the rural economy. It provided two things: timber for houses, and wood for fuel and minor constructions such as the making of hurdles. In order to produce these efficiently the coppicing system, once so characteristic of lowland England, was evolved.

A well-managed coppice contains a number of tall 'standard' trees, well-spaced and not taking much light away from the plants underneath; and a shrub layer which is regularly cut back to leave stumps which then produce long shoots. The standards provide the timber and the coppiced shrubs offer wood. As standards are felled so occasional saplings are allowed to grow through to replace them. In those few woods that are still coppiced in this traditional pattern, the shrub layer consists of a mosaic, in all stages of regrowth from the recently cut back to those parts about to be cut; this continual opening up of the ground to sunlight allows woodland plants such as primroses to flourish.

IDENTIFYING TREES

The identification of plants can seem a formidable task when you are just beginning, and the feats of those who wander around murmuring 'Salix fragilis clearly' or 'Pseudotsuga menziesii I think' may be a little unnerving. They achieve this, however, not by magic but by a process of quick categorization and elimination, and the basic rules of the game are quite easy to learn. If a botanist has no idea what a particular plant is, he uses a key to identify it with. Proper botanical keys have lists of paired questions, and one for this book might start off with:

1 Leaves small and scale-like or needle-like

Gymnosperms (Conifers) 2

1a Leaves large and/or flat, often transparent

Angiosperms (Broad-leaved trees) 50

If your tree had needles you would have a conifer and you would go to question 2, which would ask you about some other diagnostic feature. If, in contrast, statement 1a seemed more appropriate then you would have a broad-leaved tree and would skip the next 48 questions and move on to question 50.

In practice everyone can tell a pine tree from an oak, which is really all this distinction amounts to, but in doing so you have narrowed the choice of which your unknown one might be, by a very considerable margin. Becoming more skilled at identification is simply a matter of carrying a few more of these distinctions in your head, so that when you start using the book, you are roughly in the right area and have to choose from only a few possibilities.

First of all, though, you need to know what to look out for. Leaves are often good characters, in particular their size, shape, colour and the length of the stalk, but the most reliable guides are the flowers and fruit. You will soon notice that most conifers have cones rather than proper flowers, and that broad leaved trees are roughly divided into those, such as willows, poplars, oaks, and birches, that bear catkins, and those, for example apples and plums, that have what is easily recognized as a flower, large and with conspicuous petals. Pages 26–7 are a quick pictorial guide to the cones you may encounter, and pages 80–1 perform the same service for catkins.

In winter, unless you are dealing with an evergreen tree, neither leaves nor flowers are available and you will have to rely on bark and twig characters. The key on pages 20–5 is intended to help you here. Instead of a series of questions for you to work your way through, it consists of a number of boxes, each of which represents a particular combination of bark type and colour, obtained by working along the rows, and bud size and colour, found by working down the columns.

So if your leafless tree has smooth grey bark and large green buds it must be either fig, elder, or whitebeam, and the correct answer is easily checked by turning to the relevant illustrations. This sort of key is easy to use because it sets out in print the mental processes that an experienced botanist is rapidly and subconsciously going through.

Similarly you may often come across trees in full leaf that have neither flowers nor fruit and the box key on pages 16–19 will help you identify these. Once you have decided upon leaf shape and colour, you will be left with a short-list of from one to a dozen or so species to choose from. In addition, scattered through the text are some special keys to particularly difficult groups.

Mature Foliage

	Green	Dark Green
Scales	Savin 4l, Western Red Cedar 44, Coast Redwood 46	Cypresses 34–8, Phoenician Juniper 42
Needles	Giant Fir 54, Douglas Fir 58, Sitka Spruce 62, European Larch 64, Hybrid Larch 64, Deodar 66, Monterey Pine 76	Yew 30, Coast Redwood 46, Silver Fir 54, Hemlocks 60, Norway Spruce 62, Lebanon and Atlas Cedar 68, Mountain 72, Austrian 74, Shore 74, Arolla 78, and Weymouth 78
Narrow leaves	Crack and Hoary Willow 82, Osier 90, Nettle Tree 138, Wild Pear 148, Peach 170, Spindle-tree 202	Pine Bay and Almond Willow 88, Sweet Chestnut 114, Almond 168, Strawberry Tree 220, Box 204
Oval leaves	Black Poplars 96, Silver Birch 104, Apples 152, Common Lime 212, Indian Bean Tree 228	Monkey Puzzle 32, Aspen 94, Western Balsam Poplar 98, European Hop-hornbeam 108, Cultivated Apple 132
Elliptical leaves	English, Small-leaved and Fluttering Elm 134, White Mulberry 140, Cultivated Apple 152, Blackthorn 172, Cherries 166–80, Portugal Laurel 180, Oranges 188, Lemon 188, Broad leaved Spindle-tree 202, Cornelian Cherry 216	Hornbeam 108, Beech 112, Holm 128, Cork 130 and Holly 130 Oaks, Wych 132, Dutch 132 and English 134, Elm, Black Mulberry 140, Common Pear 148, Swedish and Broad-leaved Whitebeams 158, Blackthorn 172, Plums 174, Bird Cherry 118, Box 204, Rhododendron 218, Strawberry Tree 220

ellow-Green	Blue- and Grey-Green	Grey
eyland 36 and Monterey 38 ypress, White Cedar 44	Leyland Cypress 36, Wellingtonia 48	Leyland Cypress 36
panese Red Cedar 50, wamp Cypress 52, Dawn edwood 52, Giant Fir 54, eodar 66, Shore Pine 74	Swamp Cypress 52, Dawn Redwood 52, Noble Fir 56, Douglas Fir 58, Japanese and Hybrid Larch 64, Cedars 68, Stone 70, Maritime 70, Scots 72, Austrian 74, and Monterey 76 Pine	Firs (Abies) 54–8, Hemlocks 60
Weeping Willow 84, lmond 168, Peach 170	White 82 and Grey 86 Willow, Wild Pear 148, Medlar 162, Gums 214, Olive 224	Bay 88, Grey 86 and Crack 82 Willow, Sallow 86, Willow-leaved Pear 148, Gums 214
alsam Poplars 98, Cultivated pple 152, Small-leaved Lime 0, Indian Bean Tree 228	Aspen 94	
Weeping Willow 84, ommon Pear 148, Vhitebeam 158, Snowy 1espil 160, Wild Cherry176, herry Laurel 180, 1agnolias 144	Grey Alder 106, Round-leaved Oak 128, Whitebeam 158, Cornelian Cherry 216, Medlar 162	Holm 128 and Cork 130 Oak, Whitebeams 158

	Green	**Dark Green**
Rounded leaves	Downy Birch 104, Green Alder 106, Wild Pear 148, Apricot 170, Buckthorns 206, Common Lime 212	Alder 106, Hazel 110, Large-leaved Lime 212, Judas Tree 182, Holly 200
Lobed leaves	English 118 Pin 122, and Pyrenean 124 Oak, Tulip Tree 144, London Plane 146, Hawthorns 164	English 118, Durmast 120, Red 122, and Turkey 124 Oaks, Holly 200
Pinnate leaves	Rowan 154, Pagoda Tree 184, Tree of Heaven 190, Elder 230, Canary Palm 232	Black Walnut 102, Locust Tree 184, Ashes 222, Pagoda Tree 184
Trefoil leaves	Hawthorns 164, Montpelier Maple 194, London Plane 146	Fig 142, Italian Maple 196
Forked leaves	Tulip Tree 144	Gingko 28
Palmate leaves	London Plane 146, Wild Service Tree 156, Hawthorn 164 Norway 192 and Field 194 Maple, Horse Chestnut 198, Sycamore 196	Fig 142, Field 194 and Italian 196 Maple, Sycamore 196, Horse Chestnut 198

Yellow-Green	Blue- and Grey-Green	Grey
Buckthorns 206, udas Tree 182	Grey Poplar	Gums 214
Pin Oak 122	Downy Oak 126	Pyrenean Oak 124
Common Walnut 102, True Service Tree 154, Locust Tree 184, Common Ash 222, Mimosa 186,	Locust Tree 184, Date Palm 232	
Laburnums 182	Laburnums 182	
Gingko 28		
London Plane 146, Norway Maple 192	White and Grey Poplar 92	

Key to Broad-leaved Trees in Winter

Barks / Buds	Small (less than 5mm)			
	Brown and Grey	Red and Orange-Brown	Green and Green-Brown	
Smooth	Weeping Willow 84, Cornelian Cherry 216		Mimosa 186, Cornelian Cherry 216	
Flaking or Peeling	Almond Willow 88, Hawthorns 164, Italian Maple 196, Cornelian Cherry 216	Dawn Redwood 52, Crab Apple 152, Strawberry Tree 220	Birches 104, Dawn Redwood 52, Cornelian Cherry 216	
Cracked or Scarred	Hawthorns 164, Italian Maple 196	Wild Pear 148, Crab Apple 152, Box 204	Birches 40	
Ridged	Pagoda Tree 184	Judas Tree 182, Indian Bean Tree 228		

Brown, Red or Orange-Brown

Barks \ Buds	Small (less than 5mm)		
	Brown and Grey	Red and Orange-Brown	Green and Green-Brown
Smooth	Red Oak 122, Nettle Tree 138, Snowy Mespil 160, Blackthorn 172	Sallow 86, Blackthorn 172, Tree of Heaven 190	Cherry Laurel 180, Holly 200, Spindle-tree 202
Flaking or Peeling	Bird and St Lucie's Cherry 178, Hawthorns 164	Fluttering Elm 134, Field Maple 194	Birches 40, Wild Service Tree 156
Cracked or Scarred	Bay 88 and Crack 82 Willow, Italian Maple 196, Birches 104	Willow-leaved Pear 150, Field and Montpelier Maple 194	Birches 40, Wild Service Tree 156
Ridged	White and Crack Willow 82, Locust Tree 184	Crack Willow 82, Small-leaved Elm 184, Field Maple 194	Hop-hornbeam 108

White, Grey or Grey-Brown

Key to Broad-leaved Trees in Winter

| Barks | Buds | Medium 5–15mm | |
	Grey, Grey-Brown and Black	Brown	Red and Orange-Brown
Smooth	Cork Oak 130, Scotch Laburnum 182	Wild Plum 174, Peach 190, Alder Buckthorn 208	Wild Plum 174
Flaking or Peeling	Laburnum 182, Italian Maple 196	Larch 64, Buckthorn 206	Dutch Elm 132, London Plane 146, Apple 152, Hawthorns 164, Wild Cherry 176
Cracked or Scarred		English Elm 134, Cherry-plum 174	Mulberries 140, Crab Apple 152
Ridged		Honey Locust 184	Black Poplar 96, White Mulberry 140

Brown, Red or Orange-Brown

White, Grey or Grey-Brown

Medium 5–15mm

Buds / Barks	Grey, Grey-Brown and Black	Brown	Red and Orange-Brown	Green and Green-Brown
Smooth	Magnolias 144, Ashes 222	Aspen 94, Hazel 110, English Oak 118, Wild Plum 174, Cherry 196	Sallow 86, Grey and Green Alder 106, Swedish Whitebeam 158, Japanese Cherries 170, Norway Maple 192	Hornbeam 108, Hazel 110, Norway Maple 192, Sycamore 196
Flaking or Peeling	Magnolias 144, London Plane 146	Hazel 110, Medlar 162	London Plane 146, Apple 152, Medlar 162, Hawthorn 164, Japanese Cherries 170	Hazel 110, Sycamore 196,
Cracked or Scarred		Pyrenean Oak 124, Almond 168	Tulip Tree 144, Crab Apple 152, Japanese Cherries 170, Small-leaved Lime 212	Alder 106, True Service Tree 154
Ridged	Cork Oak 130, Wych Elm 132, Ashes 222	Maidenhair Tree 28, Turkey Oak 124	White and Grey Poplar 92, Sweet Chestnut 114, Small- 212 and Large-leaved Lime 210	Hornbeam 108, True Service Tree 154

Key to Broad-leaved Trees in Winter

Brown, Red or Orange-Brown

Barks \ Buds	Large (more than 5mm)		
	Brown, Grey and Black	Red and Orange-Brown	Green
Smooth			Rhododendron 218
Flaking or Peeling		Horse Chestnut 198	Larch 64
Cracked or Scarred		Horse Chestnut 198	
Ridged	Elder 230	Black Walnut 102, Elder 230	

Large (more than 15mm)

Barks \ Buds	Brown, Grey and Black	Red and Orange-Brown	Green
Smooth	Beech 112, Rowan 154, Ashes 222	Poplar 92, Balsam Poplars 98	Fig 142, Whitebeam 158, Elder 230
Flaking or Peeling		Horse Chestnut 198	
Cracked or Scarred	Beech 112	Balm of Gilead 98, Downy Oak 126, Horse Chestnut 198	
Ridged	English Oak 118, Ashes 222	Walnut 102, English 118, Durmast 120 and Downy 126 Oak, Common Lime 210	Elder 230

White, Grey or Grey-Brown

CONES

Maritime Pine, 70

Silver Fir, 54

Scots Pine, 72

Cedar of Lebanon, 6

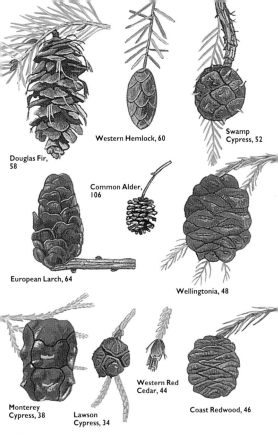

Western Hemlock, 60

Swamp Cypress, 52

Douglas Fir, 58

Common Alder, 106

European Larch, 64

Wellingtonia, 48

Monterey Cypress, 38

Lawson Cypress, 34

Western Red Cedar, 44

Coast Redwood, 46

Maidenhair Tree

Ginkgo biloba

This extraordinary primitive tree, which has no known living
relatives, was introduced from China and is now commonly planted
in parks and gardens, except in the north. Maidenhair Tree has a
fossil record stretching back 200 million years and was once
widespread throughout the northern hemisphere. Old trees can
reach 30m (**4**), but are slow-growing, and typical specimens are
10–15m, with a rather narrow, conical crown.

BARK Greyish, deeply ridged (**1**)

LEAVES Unmistakable, rather like a maidenhair fern (hence the
name), fan-shaped, split down the middle, and with veins that fork
equally (**3**). Unlike most gymnosperms it is deciduous, the leaves
falling (**5**) late to reveal green twigs, later turning brown, with small
reddish buds (**2**). The leaves are borne on stout short shoots, which
give it something of the appearance of a fruit tree in winter.

FLOWERS Rare and on separate trees, the male in yellow catkins,
the female globular on short stalks.

FRUIT Green, turning yellow brown and foul-smelling.

1

Common Yew

Taxus baccata

Yew is very long lived (to 2,000 years) and makes a massive but usually squat tree (**5**) with dark green, evergreen, flattened needles which are poisonous to cattle. Yew is widespread in central Europe, extending to Norway, western Scotland and Ireland; in England it is characteristically found on the chalk downs in the south or on limestone hills in the north and west. **Irish Yew** (**6**) which is a narrow form of Yew, or golden forms are often planted in gardens and yew trees are a familiar sight in churchyards, where the oldest specimens may pre-date the foundations of the church as yew had important pre-Christian religious significance.

BARK Reddish and flaking (**1**). The trunk is often fluted, owing to the coalescence of shoots which are repeatedly produced from its base.
LEAVES Dark green, flattened needles.
FLOWERS Male (**2**) and female flowers (**3**) are borne on separate trees, are inconspicuous, but the male trees will release clouds of pollen if knocked in early spring.
FRUIT Poisonous (**4**), pinkish-red, cup-shaped and resembles a berry, but it is actually termed an aril as it does not enclose the seed which lies at the base of the cup.

1

Monkey Puzzle or Chile Pine

Araucaria araucaria

This quite unmistakable evergreen tree is most commonly found in suburban gardens. Typical examples have a long, straight trunk, capped by whorls of spreading branches (**5**), but better-developed specimens may have more domed crowns. Monkey Puzzle was introduced from South America in the late eighteenth century, and is the only member of this genus (named after indigenous inhabitants of Chile) grown on any scale in Britain.

BARK Rough, grey or brown and shows annual growth rings (**1**).

LEAVES Twigs are made of armour-like plates each of which produces a tough, dark green, spiny leaf (**4**) and these almost completely hide the stem.

FLOWERS Male flowers (**3**) are large and cluster at the tips of stems; female flowers (**2**) appear on the same trees but take two years to ripen into fruit.

FRUIT Large spiny (**6**).

young tree

I

2

3

4

5

6

Lawson Cypress

Chamaecyparis lawsoniana

This striking, tall evergreen (**6**) from the mountains of western North America is now widely planted for both commercial and amenity purposes. Open-grown plants can reach 40m in Britain and have narrow, conical crowns with drooping tips and branches all the way down to the ground. Lawson Cypress is a fast-growing, hardy tree which is widely planted and has many varieties.

BARK Usually fissured or cracked (**1**).

LEAVES Twigs (**2**) are reddish, clothed with scale leaves and smell of parsley when crushed.

FLOWERS Male flowers red (**3**), female blue-grey (**4**); produced at the tips of the twigs in April.

FRUIT Unlike the true cypresses, the cones (**5**) mature in the same year; they are less than 1cm long and shed winged seeds.

RELATED SPECIES:

Nootka Cypress *C. nootkatensis* is another North American species but one that is much less common than Lawson Cypress, from which it differs in its smooth conical crown (**9**) yellow male flowers (**7**) and its slower-maturing fruit (**8**) which is bluer, slightly larger and more spiny. The flowers and fruit also distinguish it from the similar Leyland Cypress, p. 36.

1

2

7

3

4

5

6

8

9

Leyland Cypress

x Cupressocyparis leylandii

Although now probably the most widely planted garden evergreen, Leyland Cypress is a botanical rarity. It is a hybrid between two genera, *Cupressus* and *Chamaecyparis*, the true and false cypresses respectively, and the various types represent crosses between different pairs of species. Leyland Cypress is a tall, narrow, fast-growing and hardy tree (**6**) although, because of the phenomenal rate at which it is being planted, it is most likely to be seen as a young specimen or even as a hedge (**8**).

BARK Sometimes reddish and slightly fissured (**1**).

LEAVES Scale-like, yellow-green, green, blue-green or greyish, enclosing rather stiff shoots. The different leaf colours distinguish the various clones sold commercially, including grey (**5**), green (**4**) and blue (**7**) forms. Twigs are either flattened or branching in all planes.

FLOWERS Unusually, for a hybrid between two genera, Leyland Cypress produces both male (**2**) and female flowers.

FRUIT Female cones (**3**) about 2cm long, intermediate between the true and false cypresses.

1

Monterey Cypress

Cupressus macrocarpa

True cypresses, *Cupressus*, are distinguished from the false and hybrid cypresses (p. 36) by their larger, slow-to-mature cones and their spiky-looking twigs. Monterey Cypress is a massive, spreading tree reaching and resembling a cedar (**7**). A very fast-growing (**10**), salt-resistant tree from California that is widely planted.

BARK Brown, ridged (**1**)

LEAVES Yellowish lemon-scented scale-leaves, tightly clothing the twigs (**4**).

FLOWERS Male (**5**) small, yellow and further up the twigs than the female.

FRUIT Purple-brown cones (**6**), up to 4cm across, have 7–14 scales, each with a central boss.

RELATED SPECIES:

Italian Cypress *C. sempervirens* is a native of the Aegean, but planted all over the Mediterranean and occasionally as far north as Scotland. In cultivation characteristically pencil-shaped, but wild plants may be spreading. Its minute, dark green scale-leaves (**8**) are scentless when crushed and it has rounder, yellow-grey cones (**9**) and darker bark (**2**).

Smooth Arizona Cypress *C. glabra* is intermediate in shape, with purple-brown bark (**3**) flaking to red or yellow. This widely-planted and very hardy tree has blue-grey leaves (**11**) and purple-brown cones (**12**) which stay on the tree when ripe.

1

2

3

Common Juniper

Juniperus communis

This is the most widespread tree or shrub in Europe and one of the most variable. It ranges from the dwarf subspecies *nana* (**4**), to both columnar, even pencil-shaped forms (var. *hibernica* (**3**)) and broad and spreading forms (**5**). Usually 2–3m high, it rarely grows as high as 15m. Juniper grows in many habitats including dry mountainsides, chalk downs, and in pinewoods, but rarely in shade.

LEAVES Flattened, sharp needles (**1**) in whorls of three, grey-green to yellow-green with a broad grey band on the inner side.

FLOWERS Male and female flowers are produced on separate trees: the less numerous males in small yellow cones (**1**), the female in green cones which gradually ripen to become berries over two or three years.

FRUIT Fleshy, blue-black berries (**2**) 5–9mm across. These berries give gin its distinctive flavour.

RELATED SPECIES:

Prickly Juniper *J. oxycedrus* tends to be larger than Common Juniper and is found only in southern Europe. It can be identified by the two grey stripes on the inside of the leaves (**6**) and its large berries which measure up to 15mm and are reddish or purple-brown when ripe (**6**).

Phoenician Juniper

Juniperus phoenicea

A small tree or shrub (**2**) which differs from Common Juniper in having only scale leaves – making it look rather like a cypress – though young plants have needles too. It grows characteristically on dry, often stony hillsides and on sand dunes near the Mediterranean.

LEAVES Scales cling closely to the stem (**1**) and have a narrow papery border; the needles on young plants have two grey bands on each side.

FRUIT Male and female cones grow on the same plant, the female ripening from dark green to a rich red-brown berry 8–14mm across.

RELATED SPECIES:

Savin *J. sabina* is usually only a shrub. The immature needles grow in pairs, and the mature scales are unbordered and foul-smelling when crushed. Cones measure only 4–6mm and ripen in one year to a purplish black (**3**). It grows mainly in the mountains of central Europe.

Pencil Cedar *J. virginiana* can grow up to 30m in height (**5**). The twigs are loosely clothed with scale leaves and smell oily when crushed; needles sometimes survive on adult trees. The fruits are blue-grey when young (**4**), but brownish-violet when ripe. A native of North America, Pencil Cedar is widely planted, sometimes for timber.

Western Red Cedar

Thuja plicata

Western Red Cedar is not a true cedar but is the 'cedar' of the timber trade. It is a tall, narrowly conical, well-clothed tree (**5**), capable of 65m, but only 40m in Britain, and usually unbranched, though sometimes layering at the base to form new trunks. Its leading shoot remains upright, unlike Lawson Cypress (p. 34). It is often planted in gardens in a form with golden-striped foliage, but it is also a valuable and fast-growing timber tree, though native in North America.

BARK Dark, purplish, ridged (**1**).

LEAVES Bright-green scale-leaves (**3**), white-streaked underneath (**4**), and very aromatic.

FLOWERS Female and male flowers are found on one tree, the former conical, floppy-looking, 10–15mm, eventually rather spiny (**2**).

RELATED SPECIES:

White Cedar, *T. occidentalis*, is the most commonly planted of the other *Thuja* species. It has a more ragged crown, brighter, more flaking bark, and duller, yellowish foliage. Its scale-leaves (**6**) are not white-streaked and less strongly-scented; cones yellow, more oblong. Often planted as a yellow-leaved variety.

1

Coast Redwood

Sequoia sempervirens

In its native forests of the coastal hills of western North America, Coast Redwoods grow to over 100m: the world's tallest surviving tree is a *Sequoia* 112m high. Its characteristic oblong, rather open and untidy crown (**2**) sits on a tall, unbranched, though often suckering trunk. A very impressive and fast-growing tree, typically reaching 30–40m in Britain so far in the 150 years since it was introduced; most mature wild trees are 500–1000 years old.

BARK Soft, spongy, flaking, red-brown (**1**).

LEAVES Narrow, twisted scale-leaves clothe the stems (**4**), but bear twigs with opposite ranks of stiff, dark-green, pointed linear leaves (**3**), each with a pair of white bands underneath.

FRUIT Male cones (**6**) are yellow, on the ends of twigs, carried throughout the winter and ripening in February; female cones 20–25cm long, green and bristly, turning brown (**5**) and with widely separated scales.

Coast Redwood   Wellingtonia   1

Wellingtonia

Sequoiadendron giganteum

Wellingtonia is a shorter but more massive tree than Coast Redwood, with a neater more conical crown and lower branches that characteristically droop then turn upwards at the tip (**2**), and a massive trunk. In California trunks 25m in girth have been measured, though these are probably over 3,000 years old, while in Britain the trees have grown to 7–8m in girth over 120 years. Wellingtonia is very commonly planted in parks, at road junctions and by ambitious gardeners.

BARK Very similar to that of Coast Redwood, but brighter in young trees (**1**); it is characteristically excavated by treecreepers for roost sites.

LEAVES Strikingly different from Coast Redwood, being composed entirely of dull green or grey-green scale leaves (**3**), tightly pressed against the stem when young, but more bristly in appearance on older branches.

FRUIT Male cones are densely clustered on the youngest shoot tips and ripen in early spring; the female cones are egg-shaped and measure 5–8cm in length (**4**).

1

2

3

4

Japanese Red Cedar

Cryptomeria japonica

This attractive Japanese tree has a tall, narrow, rounded, and rather irregular crown, formed of short rising branches, giving the appearance of a conical green cumulus cloud (**2**). It reaches 30–40m in Britain, about 50m in Japan,

BARK Red-brown (**1**), darkening slowly with age and peeling in long shreds.

LEAVES In general appearance the foliage resembles Wellingtonia but it is brighter green and spiky looking. The leaves are hard, rather fleshy needles, arranged in five ranks around the twigs and shortest at the tips (**3**).

FRUIT Female cones (**4**) are spherical, 2–3cm in diameter and each scale has several short spines.

RELATED SPECIES Japanese Red Cedar is not, of course, a true cedar but a primitive relative of Wellingtonia and Coast Redwood. It grows in both China and Japan, and trees of Chinese origin have a less bushy crown and longer leaves (**5**). In gardens the most commonly encountered cultivar is 'Elegans' which is much slower growing and has a purplish tinge to the foliage.

I

Swamp Cypress

Taxodium distichum

An unmistakable tree (**7**) with a sharply narrowing, buttressed trunk, often surrounded by curious pegs or knees called pneumatophores (**8**) rising from the ground. It is a native of south-eastern North America, in swamps where the knees are thought to help the roots breathe. Swamp Cypress is often planted by water.

BARK Reddish (**1**) and fibrous as in Coast Redwood, but thinner and peeling in strips.

LEAVES Flat, linear (**5**) are grey-striped underneath and clear apple-green when young; they are arranged in two alternating ranks along side shoots which are also alternately placed. Both these shoots and the leaves are shed in the autumn (**4**).

FLOWERS Male (**3**) are produced in lumpy catkins which lengthen during the winter until they reach maturity in April.

FRUIT Small, rounded female cones (**6**) are purplish-brown when ripe.

RELATED SPECIES

Dawn Redwood *Metasequoia glyptostroboides* is a commonly planted deciduous tree, resembling a small Swamp Cypress, but with larger, paler leaves (**9**) set opposite each other on oppositely-placed side shoots, and more brightly coloured bark (**2**). It was only known as a fossil until 1948 when discovered growing wild in south-west China.

1

2

3

4

5

6

7

8

9

Common Silver Fir

Abies alba

Although not native to Britain, this is the commonest European silver fir and grows in all the central European mountains and in one area of northern France. It is now rarely planted but it was introduced early and so is widespread. It is an imposing and attractive tree (**2**) up to 50m in height, with repeated whorls of branches, making a rather ragged oblong crown which often dies back at the tip.

BARK Is smooth and grey at first but browns and cracks with age (**1**).

LEAVES Flat, rounded at the tip, are dark green above (**3**) and have a distinct midrib and two white bands underneath (**4**); they leave the shoot both horizontally and slanting upwards, but not vertically, so leaving a distinct parting (**3**).

FLOWERS Male, small, borne all over the tree.

FRUIT Cylindrical female cones (**5**) stand 10–20cm upright on the higher branches only; they are orange-brown when mature and tightly closed until disintegrating to shed seed.

RELATED SPECIES

Giant Fir *A. grandis* is now more often planted because of its rapid growth and is occasionally found self-sown. The shiny, aromatic leaves vary in length and project more or less horizontally (**6**). The cones (**7**) are smaller (5 –10cm), more rounded and red-brown.

1

Noble Fir

Abies procera

Like the Giant Fir, Noble Fir is an introduction from North America which is widely planted in western Britain. Initially the crown is neatly conical but the tree matures to produce a massive almost straight-sided crown (**2**). Noble Fir is unmistakable with its combination of massive, upright cones and blue-grey, rather bristly-looking foliage.

BARK Characteristically smooth and only slightly cracked even in old trees (**1**).

LEAVES Strikingly blue-grey and stubby, parting beneath the twig and arched up around it, giving a toothbrush effect (**3**).

FLOWERS Male, bright red when mature and the massive cones (20–25cm) are cylindrical with prominently protruding bracts arranged around it in spirals (**4**).

RELATED SPECIES:

Spanish Fir *A. pinsapo* is a curious short-needled fir that grows as a native only in a few small woods on the hills around Ronda in south Spain. Occasionally planted in gardens, it is distinguished by its dark bark, very short needles, and much shorter cones.

I

Douglas Fir

Pseudotsuga menziesii

A tall, elegant conifer providing some of the tallest trees in Britain (there are several over 50m) and holding the world height record of 127m for a tree felled in British Columbia in 1895. Vigorous trees produce a narrow open crown with horizontal branches (**2**) but more compact stunted trees are often seen. Douglas Fir is very widely planted and an extremely valuable timber tree.

BARK Dark purple-brown (**1**), thick with huge fissures.

LEAVES Aromatic, very variable in colour but are usually dull and have two white stripes beneath; they leave the shoot in all directions (**3**).

FRUIT The distinctive cones (**4**) up to 8cm long, hang from the ends of branches and have long three-toothed bracts hiding the cone scales.

RELATED SPECIES It is most likely to be confused with Silver Fir but it has more prominent reddish-brown, pointed buds, and the pendulous cones and the thick fissured bark are quite distinctive.

seed

I

Western Hemlock

Tsuga heterophylla

An elegant, conical tree (**7**) with a very characteristic drooping leading shoot and branches which point slightly upwards. Old trees lose their regular outline. This hemlock is one of several western North American trees which are now widely planted in western Europe for timber; it is particularly valuable as it can withstand deeper shade than most conifers and so can be planted under existing trees.

BARK Smooth and flaking when young, develops narrow fissures when old (**1**).

LEAVES Have a curiously irregular look as they occur in three different sizes and leave the shoot at all angles (**4** and **5**); they have rounded tips and two white bands underneath (**4**).

FRUIT Male cones (**3**) are conspicuously bright red-purple and turn white in spring, but the females (**6**) ripen to small (2–3cm), greenish-brown, neatly egg-shaped cones.

RELATED SPECIES:

Eastern Hemlock *T. canadensis* is the East Coast equivalent of Western Hemlock and so is less well suited to the European climate. It has a more untidy crown, coarsely fissured bark (**2**), smaller cones (**8**) and leaves with narrower white bands (**9**), arranged in two neat rows along the shoots. It is rarely used for forestry and mainly planted for ornament.

1

2

3

4

5

6

7

8

9

Norway Spruce

Picea abies

This is the true Christmas tree and the native European spruce, although introduced into Britain. Its crown is very regular and conical with more-or-less level branches often turned up at the tips (**5**). Norway Spruce forms huge natural forests in the European mountains and is widely planted for timber and Christmas sales (**6**).

BARK Usually has a slight reddish tinge and is thin, rough and cracked (**1**).

LEAVES Stiff, sharp needles; pale green when first produced but soon turn a deep dark green; they lie half-flattened against the stem and except for a small gap on the under side cover the stem densely (**2**). When they fall they leave a characteristic 'peg' (**4**).

FRUIT Spruce cones (**3**) are up to 18cms long, cylindrical and always hang downwards.

RELATED SPECIES:

Sitka Spruce *P. sitchensis* is a native of western North America that flourishes in western Europe in areas of high rainfall, reaching 50m, and is now probably the commonest tree in Britain. It is the fastest growing tree on wet, peaty, upland soils and so has been planted in millions for forestry; in addition spontaneous seedlings often occur. It is distinguished by its flattened, bluish, even sharper needles (**7**) and its much smaller, more rounded, pale brown cones.

1

2

3

4

5

6

7

European Larch

Larix decidua

Larches are much the commonest winter-bare conifers – the others are Dawn Redwood and Swamp Cypress – and are easily distinguished by their knobbly twigs (**1**). European Larch is an elegant tree (**3**) with down-sweeping branches turning upwards (some times vertically) at the tips; it can reach 45m in cultivation but 30–35m is more usual in the wild.

BARK Grey or brown, breaking into long fissures (**2**).

LEAVES Limp, bright-green needles, borne in neat tufts (**4**) from late March to October, when they fall golden-brown, on special 'short shoots' (the knobs) which never elongate.

FLOWERS Male (**6**) and female (**7**) cones are often borne on the same twig: the females are feathery and purplish-red; the males are less than 1cm long, bright yellow with a purplish ring round the base, and shedding pollen in April.

FRUIT The mature cone (**5**) is egg-shaped, smooth, less than 4cm long and will often remain on the tree for years.

RELATED SPECIES:

JAPANESE LARCH *L. kaempferi* has dull orange-brown (not yellowish) twigs, flatter, greyer needles, and cones (**8**) with outward pointing scales. It is a native of Japan and like the hybrid between these, Hybrid Larch *L. x marschlinsii* which is intermediate in most characters (**9**), is planted more than *L. decidua* because of its very rapid growth rate

1

2

Deodar

Cedrus deodara

Cedars are massive evergreen trees with tufts of needles borne on special 'short shoots', as in the larches. Deodar is an attractive, conical tree (**2**) with a drooping main shoot and lower branches often sweeping down to ground level, obscuring the trunk. A native of the Himalayas, this fast-growing tree is now very commonly planted usually for ornament, occasionally for timber. It is best distinguished from the other cedars by its drooping main shoot and longer needles

BARK Trunk is dark, smooth or finely cracked (**1**).

LEAVES Needles are longer than those of other cedars (3–4cm) and are initially borne in a widely-spaced spiral on young twigs, and then in tufts (**3**).

FLOWERS The long, cylindrical, slightly curved male cones are conspicuously purple when mature in autumn; female cones (**4**) are tightly egg-shaped, with the scales pressed closely against each other, maturing to a length of 10–14cm over two or three years and then disintegrating.

1

Cedar of Lebanon

Cedrus libani

A massive, squat, almost flat-topped tree (**4**) whose trunk can reach enormous dimensions and is usually complicatedly branched to give a pillar-like effect. The upper branches are normally almost level, the lower ones often drooping and giving a strange effect of dense patches of foliage pierced by large gaps. Cedar of Lebanon is now extremely rare in its native Near East, but is often planted for dramatic effect rather than ornament.

BARK Typically dull grey-brown with long sinuous ridges (**2**).

LEAVES Needles (**3**) are shorter, stiffer and usually duller green than a Deodar's.

FLOWERS Male cones are greyish and 5cm long; the female cones are similar to the Deodar's but slightly pointed at the tip and pinkish-brown when mature (**5**).

RELATED SPECIES:

Atlas Cedar *C. atlantica* is readily identifiable in its common blue form *glauca*, (**6**), but mature green trees are difficult to distinguish from Cedar of Lebanon. However, young trees have upward-pointing tips to all shoots, and even older, flatter trees usually retain a trace of a point; in addition the 'short shoots' are longer and the cone (**1**) is smaller. This cedar is a native of the Atlas mountains of North Africa.

I

2

3

5

4

6

Stone Pine

Pinus pinea

One of the most characteristic sights of the Mediterranean coast are
the groves of Stone Pines (**7**), with their domed crowns casting
much valued shade. Although salt-resistant and much planted on the
Mediterranean coast, Stone Pine is frost-sensitive and is therefore
scarce further north.

BARK Orange-brown (**2**), with a few deep vertical cracks.

LEAVES Long (10–20cm) greyish needles in pairs (**6**).

FLOWERS Male cones (**3**) are small and orange; the female (**5**)
matures into a large, rounded, rather shiny, rich brown cone (**4**),
which sheds an economically valuable crop of edible, wingless seeds.

RELATED SPECIES:

Maritime Pine *P. pinaster* is another Mediterranean coastal pine
but with a taller, more open, rather straggly crown. The mature
cones (**1**) are much narrower and more conical than in Stone Pine
and may stay on the tree for several years before opening. The trunk
can be tapped for resin.

1

2

Scots Pine

Pinus sylvestris

This is the only native British pine and it is found throughout Europe, though only in the mountains in the south. It is a tall tree (**6**), capable of 35–40m. Scots Pine is an extremely variable tree, growing wild in Scotland in rather open forests with a rich ground flora, and widely naturalized on heaths in England and Wales, when young seedlings (**1**) may be common. It is also often planted both for timber and ornament. The Scottish race has a very conical crown (**7**) and develops the mature shape (**6**), more flat-topped, late; other races remain conical always

BARK Characteristic colouring (**2**) on the upper part of the trunk, ranging from rusty brown to orange, and cracked into small, smooth plates.

LEAVES Fat, blue-grey needles are 3–7cm long and borne in pairs.

FLOWERS The male cones (**3**) are conspicuous as a yellow cluster around the base of the young shoot in May, but soon fall. The female cones (**4**) are initially green, but mature in the third year to give a greyish, oval cone, 4–7cm long (**5**).

RELATED SPECIES:

Mountain Pine *P. mugo* is almost a shrub, forming scrub at high altitudes in the Alps. The needles (**8,9**) are also in pairs. It is often planted.

3

4

5

6

7

8

9

Austrian Pine

Pinus nigra ssp *nigra*

A magnificent tall pine with a very densely-branched crown (**4**). The crown is usually conical, though rather irregular, appearing very dark green or almost black from a distance. Austrian Pine is a native of the mountains of central Europe but is now widely planted for ornament and shelter, especially on calcareous soils.

BARK Very dark (**2**).

LEAVES Paired, straight and very dark green when young (**1**) but curve inwards and turn almost black with age (**5**); the buds have long pointed tips.

FLOWERS Cones (**6**, **7**) are 5–8cm long, suggesting lopsided Scots Pine cones.

RELATED SPECIES:

Corsican Pine, ssp *laricio* is preferred for its superior timber outside central Europe, and where planted for forestry. Corsican pine is distinguished by its flexible, twisted needles, longer and paler than in Austrian Pine, and its blunter buds. Huge forests of Corsican Pine can be seen, for example, near Thetford and on the Culbin Sands. Male flowers (**3**) are also illustrated.

Lodgepole Pine *P. contorta* is a North American pine which has been planted widely in north and west Britain, at high altitudes and on particularly infertile soils. It has greener foliage (**8**) very short needles (3–6cm), and small, prickly cones (**9**).

1

2

3

4

5

6

7

8

9

Monterey Pine

Pinus radiata

This tall, bulky pine with a rounded crown (**5**) hails from a few coastal regions of California and is often planted near western coasts in Britain, where its wind-resistance is its main asset.

BARK Has deep vertical channels and flakes into intricate patterns (**2**).

LEAVES Needles (**1**,**4**) are in threes, and are bright green, long (10–15cm) and thin, giving the branches a rather delicate appearance.

FLOWERS Monterey Pine has unique cones (**6**) that are retained on the tree and so are always present as a diagnostic feature: they are large, up to 14cm long, and one-sidedly protuberant at the base, owing to the enlargement of the knobs of the cone-scales. Male flowers (**3**) are also illustrated.

Related species:

Ponderosa Pine *P. ponderosa* is another three-needled pine but with even longer (20cm), dull grey-green needles (**7**). It has a narrower crown, scaly, pinkish or yellowish bark, and mature cones which are slightly smaller (8–12cm) and faintly prickly when mature.

1

2

3

4

5

6

7

Arolla Pine

Pinus cembra

Arolla Pine is one of the commoner of the planted pines which have needles in groups of fives. It is usually seen as rather a small tree (rarely over 20m) with a dense, narrow crown (**3**), and it is commonest in northern Europe. In the wild it grows in central Europe at high altitudes, often right up to the tree-line.

BARK Gently ridged and scaly.

LEAVES Short (5–8cm) needles (**1**) are dark green on one side and greyish-white on the other, and are borne in dense tufts, on twigs covered with brown fur.

FRUIT Short, squat cones (**2**), bluey-green at first but ripen to a russet brown.

RELATED SPECIES:

Weymouth Pine *P. strobus* is another 5-needled pine but its needles (**4**) are up to 12–14cm long. It is a much taller tree, once widely planted as an introduction from eastern North America, and when mature has a rounded crown. It has long but very narrow cones (**4**), often curved at the tip, and hanging from branches.

Arolla Pine

Weymouth Pine

1

2

3

4

Maidenhair, 28

Sycamore, 196

White Poplar, 92

♂

Black Poplar, 96

♂

Aspen, 9[

♀

Walnut, 10[

Hazel, 110

Sweet Chestnut, 114

Hornbeam, 108

♂

Silver Birch, 104

♂

CATKINS

Swamp Cypress, 52

English Oak, 118

Beech, 112

♂ Bay Willow, 88

♂ Crack Willow, 82

♀

Almond Willow, 88

Hop-hornbeam, 108

Sallow, 86

Common Alder, 106

White Willow

Salix alba

White Willow is a tall, straggly tree reaching 15–20m with long, steeply ascending branches hidden by the striking, dense, silvery-grey foliage (**7**). White Willow is widespread throughout Europe, though introduced in the north, and found in all parts of Britain. A characteristic riverside tree in lowland areas, it is frequently pollarded on river banks to give an ugly stumpy trunk with tall, narrow ascending shoots.

BARK Grey-brown, deeply fissured (**3**).

LEAVES Long and narrow, tapering to curled tips, and are hairy beneath (**6**).

FLOWERS Catkins are long and narrow; the males (**4**) have two stamens and are bright yellow in April, while the females (**5**) are green, turning white and fluffy as the downy seeds are shed in June. The buds are long and tightly pressed against the twigs (**1**).

VARIETIES Several are grown, including **Golden Osier** var. *vitellina* (p. 84) with striking yellow twigs, and var. *coerulea*, the Cricket Bat Willow, which has a tighter crown and bluish leaves; it is grown for making cricket bats.

RELATED SPECIES:

Crack Willow *S. fragilis* has more spreading branches, brighter green leaves (**8**), and twigs (**2**) that readily break and take root. A confusing range of hybrids are found wherever both parents occur. Male (**9**) and female (**10**) catkins are also illustrated.

Weeping Willow

Salix x sepulcralis

Weeping Willow shares with Monkey Puzzle the distinction of being the easiest tree to identify in Britain; however, there are several types of Weeping Willow whose nomenclature and identification is less simple. The most commonly planted type (**5**) is the hybrid between Golden Osier and the Chinese *S. babylonica* known as *S. x sepulcralis*. It has characteristic long, curved, drooping shoots reaching to the ground and clothed in narrow, softly hairy leaves (**4**); bright yellow twigs (**1**); and usually only male catkins (**3**) which are yellow and curved upwards.

RELATED SPECIES:

The parent, *Salix babylonica*, is much rarer and has brown twigs and shorter catkins. Other hybrids occur with White Willow or Crack Willow instead of Golden Osier: these all weep and have some of the characters of the parents.

Golden Osier *S. alba* var. *vitellina* (**6**) is a variety of White Willow (p. 82) and one of two parents of the hybrid Weeping Willow. It is grown for its brilliant yellow twigs (**2**) which are straighter. Its leaves and catkins resemble White Willow.

1

2

3

4

5

6

Sallow or Pussy Willow

Salix caprea

Sallow normally forms a large bush but it can produce a respectable trunk and crown up to about 10m (**8**) particularly when growing in woodland. Its branches ascend from a smooth or widely cracked trunk and the twigs (**1**) are quite smooth. Common throughout northern Europe, except in the south west, in damp and dry woods and scrub.

BARK Can be smooth or widely cracked (**3**).

LEAVES More rounded than any other tree-forming willow, less than twice as long as broad; they are dark green and wrinkled above (**7**), grey and silky beneath (**6**).

FLOWERS Male trees are dramatically recognizable in March and April when the large bright yellow catkins (**5**) are in flower; the female trees bear longer (up to 7cm) silky-green catkins (**4**) which explode in May liberating white cottony seeds.

RELATED SPECIES:

Grey Willow *S. cinerea* is almost always a shrub, but small trees can be recognized by the slightly hairy twigs (**2**), which have small ridges under the bark, and the narrower leaves (**9**), about twice as long as broad. Both subspecies *cinerea* and *oleifolia* (recognized by the rusty-red hairs under the leaves) occur in Britain, although the latter is more common; usually in wetter places than Sallow. Catkins (**10**) are also illustrated.

1

2

3

Almond Willow

Salix triandra

Almond Willow was once widely planted as an osier, when its typical form is a mass of long, ascending shoots rising from a stumpy base, this being the best method of producing the long canes required for basketwork. If left uncut, trees of 10–12m can be seen, somewhat like White Willow in shape. Though well distributed in much of Europe, except in the far north and west, the Almond Willow is often overlooked, and usually found in abandoned osier beds in marshy valleys, and in fens.

BARK Characteristic; flaking, smooth (1).
LEAVES Long, narrow, hairless (3), about five times as long as broad.
FLOWERS Bright yellow male catkins (4), each flower in which has three stamens, and which are very conspicuous in April.

RELATED SPECIES:
Bay Willow *S. pentandra* is usually smaller, even when in tree form. It has fissured bark (2), sticky-looking buds, and more rounded, bay-scented leaves (only about three times as long as broad) dark glossy green above (6) and paler below. It has conspicuous female catkins (7) and the striking male catkins (5) appear in May after the leaves and have five or more stamens in each flower. A characteristic northern and upland plant of lake, streamsides, and moorlands

1

2

♀

3

4

5

6

7

Osier

Salix viminalis

Osiers are a quite unmistakable feature of lowland Britain, with their immensely long branches (**4**), often arising from pruned stools. Osiers occur naturally by stream-sides and in fens and marshes, and along with many hybrids were formerly extensively planted in special osier beds in wet valleys, now usually degenerated into dense thickets. Common throughout lowland Britain and most of the Continent.

LEAVES Narrow (**1**), 10–15 times as long as broad, which are white with short, silky hairs underneath, and spread almost horizontally.

FLOWERS Catkins are rather inconspicuous, produced in April and May with the leaves, and on very short stalks, so that they tend to be hidden by the long leaves; the male catkins (**3**) are rather stubby and usually only about 3cm long, but the female (**2**) are longer and more cylindrical.

RELATED SPECIES:

S. elaeagnos is another very narrow-leaved willow from central Europe, particularly along river banks in the Alps. It has very narrow, curved catkins. One form, with leaves (**5**) so fine that it has the air of a Tamarisk, is often cultivated.

pruned stools

White Poplar

Populus alba

The poplars are a puzzling group and it is hard to say which are the true species and where they are native. White Poplar is certainly introduced in Britain and is probably a native of south and east Europe. It forms a medium-sized, little-branched, rather untidy crown (**5**). White Poplar is wind-resistant and suckers freely, so that it is much planted near the sea, particularly to stabilize loose sand.

BARK Dark grey-brown, ridged bark (**2**). The bark of young trees is whitish with dark marks.

LEAVES Deeply-lobed leaves (**3**) which are dull green on the top and white underneath; young twigs (**1**) are ridged and white-downy.

FLOWERS Catkins (**4**) are very conspicuous in March and early April, the males bright reddish-purple with grey hairs and up to 10cm long, the females greenish with well-separated flowers.

RELATED SPECIES:

Grey Poplar *P. x canescens* is a larger tree with less deeply-lobed leaves (**6**) which are greyish, not white, underneath. It is probably a hybrid between White Poplar and Aspen (p.94) and is rather more common than the former.

1

2

Aspen

Populus tremula

The most widespread and the smallest European poplar, rarely exceeding 15m. Aspen (**4**) is not only widespread geographically, extending from the Arctic to the Mediterranean and right across Asia, but also ecologically. It is most commonly found in wet woods, hedges and screes and on moorland, often in company with Downy Birch (p. 104). In woods its presence is betrayed by its slow-to-rot leaves, which remain yellow in the leaf litter throughout the winter.

BARK Smooth silvery-green bark (**2**) which eventually turns brown or greyish. Twigs are slightly glossy (**1**).

LEAVES Instantly recognizable, almost circular, gently scalloped (**3**), flutter from side to side in the lightest breeze on long leaf stalks. Heart shaped, untoothed leaves are borne on sucker shoots which grow up around the tree and often form extensive thickets.

FLOWERS Before the leaves appear the male trees produce silky, dumpy catkins (**6**), 4–8cm long; female trees have green catkins (**5**) which turn white in May when the woolly seeds are shed (**7**).

1

2

3

4

5

6

7

Black Poplar

Populus nigra

The black poplars are a confusing group distinguished by their dark, deeply furrowed bark (**2**), finely toothed leaves and almost hairless catkins. The true European Black Poplar ssp. *betulifolia* is not often seen now but can be instantly recognized by its floppy, rather ungainly crown (**7**), reaching 30–35m and its massive trunk broken by protruding bosses. Black Poplar may be native in damp woods and by streams in southern England; elsewhere it is found south to the Mediterranean, but the hybrids and varieties below are more often planted.

BARK Dark, deeply furrowed bark with protruding bosses (**2**).

LEAVES Bright green, glossy (**5**) with distinctive clear borders and long, stiff stalks.

FLOWERS Flat buds (**1**) and male trees bear masses of bright red catkins (**4**) in April, before the leaves; the female catkins (**6**) are longer and have widely spaced flowers.

RELATED SPECIES:

Lombardy Poplar *P. nigra* var. *italica* has an unmistakable slim outline (**8**). It is always male, has bark with no bosses and is widely planted. Several similar varieties occur.

Black Italian Poplar *P.* x *canadensis* var. *serotina* (**9**) is easily confused with Black Poplar but it is usually larger, has no bosses on its trunk (**3**) and a neater crown, with upward growing branches. A hybrid between *P. nigra* and the American *P. deltoides*, it is widely planted for timber and ornament.

Balm of Gilead

Populus x jackii

Balm of Gilead is one of the most widely planted of an extremely confusing group of poplars, known as balsam poplars because of the powerful smell emitted by their fat, sticky buds in spring, and detectable from considerable distances. It is a very fast-growing tree, occasionally reaching 30m (**5**) but most often seen as a smaller, neat conical crown, surrounded by suckers (**6**). It is probably a hybrid between two North American poplars – Eastern Balsam Poplar or Tacamahac, *P. balsamifera*, and Cottonwood, *P. deltoides* – both of which are also sometimes planted here. It is often planted on industrial waste land and is sometimes called *P. candicans*, particularly when sold in a variegated form. Tacamahac produces both male and female catkins (**3**).

BARK Greyish, cracked (**2**) and its twigs (**1**) are stout, hairy, and slightly angled.

LEAVES Pale green above and yellowish below, hairy on the veins and somewhat ace-of-spades shaped (**4**).

FLOWERS As a hybrid it has no male catkins, only long green female ones, and reproduces by suckering.

RELATED SPECIES:

Western Balsam Poplar *P. trichocarpa* is also from North America, but less often planted. It lacks suckers, but has very angled twigs and leaves (**7**) with straighter bases.

1

2

3

4

5

7

6

NUTS

Walnut, 102

Horse Chestnut, 198

English Oak, 118

London Plane, 146

Beech, 112

Sweet Chestnut, 114

Hazel, 110

WINGED FRUITS

Sycamore, 196

English Elm, 134

Hornbeam, 108

Ash, 222

Tree of Heaven, 190

Silver Birch, 104

Tulip Tree, 144

Common Walnut

Juglans regia

A superb tree, introduced for its delicious fruit from south-east Europe, probably as early as the fifteenth century. Typically Walnuts are grown as single specimen trees, in parks, gardens, or hedgerows, where they produce an expansive crown (**8**), with spreading low branches, but rarely exceed 20m. Widely grown for fruit and timber and occasionally naturalized, Walnut is most recognizable in spring when the leaves open a rich orange.

BARK The trunk can be massive with wide, smooth, grey plates separated by deep fissures (**3**) and the twigs (**2**) are rather thick.

LEAVES Strikingly large (**4**) and have 7–9 pairs of pointed, leathery, rather dull green leaflets, each up to 15cm long, giving a general impression of a rather overgrown ash leaf, and strongly scented.

FLOWERS Male flowers (**6**) in drooping catkins; female flowers (**7**) in small, inconspicuous groups at the tips of shoots.

FRUIT Female flowers ripen to a large green fruit (**1**), 5cm across; inside this lies the famous wrinkled nut (**5**).

RELATED SPECIES:
Black Walnut *J. nigra* is an American walnut, less often encountered, and immediately recognized by its dark, deeply ridged bark, and its lighter green, more delicate leaves (**9**), each with about 15 leaflets.

3

4

5

6

7

9

8

Silver Birch

Betula pendula

An elegant, fast-growing tree, rarely surviving
more than 100 years, found throughout almost all
Europe, and distinguished by its drooping twigs,
hanging down from stiffly held main branches (**7**).
Capable of reaching 30m, though rarely seen above
20m, Silver Birch starts out as a neat conical tree.
Silver Birch is a common and characteristic tree of
dry, sandy and peaty soils, often seen colonizing
heather moor.

BARK Pinkish-brown in young trees, later white,
scaly (**1**), with conspicuous black patches.

LEAVES Oval with a long pointed tip (**6**),
obviously toothed, but with smaller teeth in
between those formed by the main veins.

FLOWERS Male catkins (**4**) are 4–5cm long,
drooping, yellowish, in small groups; female catkins
(**3**) are shorter, green at first in spring and upright,
later drooping and turning brown (**5**)

FRUIT Female catkins shed masses of tiny winged
seeds (**8**) in autumn. Each seed has two papery
wings, more than twice as wide as the seed.

RELATED SPECIES:

Downy Birch *B. pubescens* has grooved, greyish
bark (**2**), not marked as Silver Birch, and spreading
branches (**10**). Leaves (**9**) have an abrupt pointed
tip and only one row of teeth. The wings of the
seeds (**11**) are narrower. As common as Silver
Birch, it prefers wetter soils. Hybrids are common.

Common Alder

Alnus glutinosa

One of the commonest waterside trees, Alder rarely reaches 20m, though in cultivation it is capable of 40m. When young, it has an unusually regular conical shape for a non-conifer, but mature trees have rather open, straggly crowns (**7**).

BARK Grey or brown, with a fine network of shallow fissures (**1**).

LEAVES Strikingly rounded (**6**), somewhat resembling Hazel (p. 110), but often with an indented tip; bright green and rather shiny, with 4–7 pairs of veins.

FLOWERS Male catkins (**4**) are rather like those of the birches, but strikingly contrast purple scales with yellow flowers. Female catkins (**5**) distinguish Alders from all other similar trees, being cone-like (**3**) and remaining on the tree (**2**) long after the tiny winged seeds are shed.

RELATED SPECIES:

Grey Alder *A. incana* is a European tree, absent only from the north-west, but often planted in land reclamation schemes on colliery spoil heaps. It has smooth, grey bark and pointed, oval leaves (**8**), strongly toothed and greyish beneath. Hybrids with Common Alder occur.

Green Alder *A. viridis* grows mainly in the Alps and in south-east Europe. It has leaves (**9**) intermediate in shape, and catkins in small groups, appearing with the leaves.

1

Hornbeam

Carpinus betulus

An attractive tree reaching 30m with steeply ascending branches, often producing a crown widest near the top. Young trees are more conical, but short specimens are more likely to have been pollarded (**7**). Found in much of Europe, but not in the north and west. Locally common in south-east England, where it forms pure woods, and widely planted elsewhere. Often found as an understorey tree in oakwood.

BARK Smooth, greyish (**1**), sometimes fissured and always buttressed.

LEAVES Rather like those of beech, but with very prominent parallel veins and strongly toothed margins (**6**).

FLOWERS Male borne in attractive, short, greenish, rather feathery catkins (**4**).

FRUIT Female catkins (**3**) are very characteristic, short and green, but elongating in fruit, to give instantly recognizable clusters, with each fruit on a 3-lobed wing (**5**).

RELATED SPECIES:

Hop-hornbeam *Ostrya carpinifolia* is a southern European tree, occasionally planted. It is recognized by its hop-like clusters of very pale yellowish-green fruits (**8**) and finely cracked bark (**2**).

1

2

Hazel

Corylus avellana

Hazel is not strictly a tree if we adhere to the requirement for a single trunk, for it almost invariably produces a dense mass of long arching branches (**6**). If left uncut, however, it is capable of producing a trunk and of reaching 8–10m. It is easily recognized at all times of year: in winter by its growth form, its almost yellowish-brown twigs (**1**), and its conspicuous green, rounded buds and immature catkins. Hazel is a very widely distributed shrub in Europe, found all over the British Isles and absent only from the mountains of Scandinavia. In Britain it forms a characteristic shrub layer in oak woods, especially where coppiced to produce the long new twigs for hurdles, wattles, basketry, and the like, but is quite capable of reaching the canopy where the trees are poorly grown. In the extreme west of Britain, especially on sea-cliffs, Hazel forms pure stands, usually shrubby and wind-cut.

LEAVES Characteristic of Hazel in summer; round, pointed-tipped leaves (**3**), with softly prickly hair.

FLOWERS Distinctive in spring; familiar yellow male catkins (**2**), 4–7cm long, and maturing at any time from Christmas onwards.

FRUIT Familiar in autumn; clusters of 1–4 nuts (**4**), initially green, but turning brown (**5**) when ripe, and fringed by conspicuous frilly bracts.

1

2

3

4

5

6

Beech

Fagus sylvatica

An impressive tree, reaching 30–40m with an enormous, spreading crown (**10**). Native from Spain to south Norway and southern England and often planted further north. Dominant on chalk and some well-drained sands in north-west Europe, but in central Europe more of a mountain tree, forming forests with oak or spruce. Its wood is used for furniture and many ornamental varieties are planted, e.g. Copper Beech.

BARK Trunk is smooth and grey (**2**), (though mostly green with algae), often branching almost horizontally.

LEAVES Pointed oval, with veins protruding at the edges. Young leaves are silky underneath, delicate yellow-green (**3**), quickly turning shiny dark green (**5**) and finally rich brown by late autumn (**9**); young trees and hedges retain dead leaves in autumn. Twigs are brown, slightly flexuous, bearing characteristic narrow, pointed buds (**7**)

FLOWERS Male flowers borne in small, rounded catkins, hanging on long stalks (**6**), the females in short-stalked, erect clusters (**4**).

FRUIT Nut is almost pyramidal, glossy brown, and protected by a tough coat (the mast, **8**) which splits into 4 sections and then germinates (**1**) in large numbers the following spring.

3

4

5

6

7

8

9

10

Sweet Chestnut

Castanea sativa

A handsome and striking tree, frequently
growing to about 30m, Sweet Chestnut was
almost certainly introduced by the Romans who
relied heavily on its nuts and even made flour
from them. Although a vigorous tree in Britain,
especially on light sandy soils, it has naturalized
in surprisingly few places. It forms an even, well-
structured crown (**6**) with rather few, but
massive spreading branches.

BARK Quite characteristic with deep, spiral,
parallel ridges which usually twist sharply near
the ground (**2**). Twigs (**1**) bear large squat buds.

LEAVES Narrow, dark green, sharply-toothed,
glossy (**3**); among the longest of any tree to be
found in Britain (up to 25cm).

FLOWERS Produces catkins later than most
other trees, on stiff, upright stalks bearing widely
spaced male flowers (**5**) and a few small spiky
female flowers at the base (**4**). As female flowers
mature into fruit the male flowers wither but the
brown stalk of the catkin projects from the
cluster.

FRUIT Female flowers mature into the
characteristic green, spiky chestnut fruit (**7**).
Each fruit usually has two tough-skinned but
richly flavoured nuts (**8**) which unfortunately
only mature in favourable years in Britain.

1

2

English, 118

Durmast, 120

Turkey, 124

Red, 122

Pin, 122

OAK LEAVES AND NUTS
(ACORNS)

Holm, 128

Cork, 130

Pyrenean, 124

Holly, 130

Downy, 126

Round-leaved, 128

English Oak

Quercus robur

Common throughout Europe, except the far
north, and the most important forest tree of
north-west Europe, English Oak is extremely
variable in size and shape, sometimes producing
tall, rather ragged crowns, in extreme cases up
to 45m high, but more usually a massive, twisted
dome (**8**) often less than 20m high when
mature. This is because the leading shoot dies
(or is eaten); the side shoots then grow off in a
different direction, giving branches with a
succession of dog-legs. Oak forms extensive
woods on heavy land, being replaced by Alder in
wet valleys and on dry soils by Beech in the
south and Ash, Birch or Pine in the north. In the
English Midlands it reigns supreme.

BARK Grey (**2**), is finely cracked and ridged.
The twigs (**3**) bear rounded but pointed buds.

LEAVES Very short-stalked, but deeply lobed
(**6**), with two small backward-pointing lobes at
the base.

FLOWERS Male catkins (**4**) are conspicuous in
short clusters in early May as the leaves unfold;
the female catkins (**5**) are similar, but shorter
and bearing minute flowers.

FRUIT The familiar acorn (**7**), in small clusters
on long stalks; jays and squirrels bury them in
hoards, so that groups of seedlings (**1**) are
sometimes seen.

Durmast or Sessile Oak

Quercus petraea

Durmast Oak is a very similar tree to English Oak, but rarely forms the massive, low crowns of the latter; it is less prone to zigzag growth so is, typically, a taller, straighter, more elegant tree (**5**). Durmast Oak largely replaces English Oak as the main forest tree on the thinner, acid soils of northern and western Britain, and its woods tend for this reason to be much poorer in associated plants and insects. Indeed, while English Oak is sometimes stripped of leaves by the caterpillars of various moths, particularly the Winter Moth, Mottled Umber, and Green Tortrix, the same fate rarely befalls Durmast Oak.

BARK Has longer, straighter fissures (**1**) and tends to be less cracked than English Oak. Best distinguished from English Oak by its grey-purple twigs (**2**).

LEAVES Long-stalked (**7**), lacking the small, backward-pointed lobes, and tapering smoothly onto the stalk.

FLOWERS Male catkins (**4**) are longer than in English Oak, and the female flowers (**3**) are inconspicuous in the leaf axils.

FRUIT Acorns are unstalked in Sessile Oak (**6**) – i.e., the stalk is on the leaves in Durmast Oak and on the acorns in English Oak.

1

Red Oak

Quercus rubra

Red Oak is a widely planted North American tree, valuable both economically for its timber and aesthetically for its superb, brilliant orange-red autumn colouring (**7**). Although it is capable of reaching 30–35m, it usually only reaches 20–25m in Britain.

BARK Trunk is straight, smooth and silvery (**2**); a winter twig (**1**) is also illustrated. Branches are massive and spreading (**8**).

LEAVES More deeply lobed (**5**) than in most other oaks, and have fine points at the tips of the lobes.

FLOWERS Male flowers (**4**) are borne in conspicuous, slender, yellowish catkins, but the female flowers (**3**) are well-hidden at the base of the leaves and mature over two years.

FRUIT Female flowers mature to produce a rather rounded acorn (**6**) which sits in a characteristically wide, shallow cup.

RELATED SPECIES:

Pin Oak *Q. palustris* is a similar North American tree, less frequently encountered than the Red Oak, and distinguished from it by its even more deeply lobed leaves (**9**), which have an almost feathery appearance and turn bright scarlet in autumn. It also has somewhat drooping twigs, conspicuous tufts of hairs on the leaves where the veins branch, and smaller (10–15mm) acorn cups. Pin Oak is mainly planted for timber in central Europe and for ornament in Britain.

4

5

6

7

8

9

Turkey Oak

Quercus cerris

An elegant, long-lived tree that produces a tall, domed crown (**5**), usually borne on a long, straight, unbranched trunk. Turkey Oak can be distinguished from other oaks by the long narrow filaments that surround its leaf buds and which persist to form stipules at the base of the leaves (**4**). Introduced from south-east Europe it is frequently planted and is fully naturalized in southern England, mainly on dry, sandy soils.

BARK Coarsely-fissured grey (**2**), showing orange in the cracks. A winter twig (**1**) is also illustrated.

LEAVES Dark, dull green, usually hairy underneath, and with deep, regular, near-triangular lobes (**4**).

FLOWERS Male flowers are produced in dense clusters of dull yellow catkins (**3**).

FRUIT The oblong acorns in their characteristic bristly, unstalked cups take two years to ripen (as in Red Oak) and so are mature on the old twigs, not on the new growth.

RELATED SPECIES:

Pyrenean Oak *Q. pyrenaica* is a suckering tree with narrower leaf lobes (**6**), and white down on the leaf undersides. It is late into leaf and produces masses of golden-yellow male catkins and scaly, short-stalked acorns (**7**). Rarely planted, Pyrenean Oak is a native of southern Europe and naturalized in Belgium.

1

2

Downny Oak

Quercus pubescens

A widespread native tree in central Europe, Downy Oak can reach 20–25m (**5**), but usually only does so in collections or gardens. It is most often encountered as a tall shrub (**6**), and in many respects it resembles a rather depauperate Durmast Oak (p. 120). It is a characteristic small tree or shrub forming low woods on dry, south-facing limestone hillsides primarily in south-east Europe, but scattered north to France, Belgium and Germany, where it is usually accompanied by hybrids with Durmast Oak and sometimes with English Oak as well, making identification difficult. It is occasionally planted in parks.

BARK Grey, ridged (**2**). Has characteristic long grey hairs on its twigs (**1**).

LEAVES Shallow lobes only (**4**), covered with dense short hairs underneath, at least in the early part of the season.

FLOWERS Male flowers (**3**) are in catkins like those of other oaks.

FRUIT Acorns (**7**) are egg-shaped and borne in small, slightly hairy cups on very short stalks.

3

4

5

6

7

Holm Oak

Quercus ilex

This is the most frequently encountered evergreen oak in Northern Europe, forming a widely-spreading dome up to 25m high (**5**). Holm Oak is a common Mediterranean tree, native as far north as Brittany, and widely planted elsewhere, becoming naturalized in southern England.

BARK Dark grey-brown, almost black from afar, and finely cracked (**1**).

LEAVES Evergreen, maturing from shining bright green (**4**), through dull green to a very dark colour before being eventually shed; long and narrow, with whitish short hairs underneath and no lobes, except on sucker shoots (**6**).

FLOWERS Male (**2**) are borne in long yellow catkins, conspicuous against the dark foliage.

FRUIT Acorns (**3**) are egg-shaped and sit well-exposed in the grey-hairy cup, ripening between May and September.

RELATED SPECIES:

Round-leaved Oak *Q. rotundifolia* is a smaller tree with broader, rather greyish leaves (**7**), found in south-west Europe.

1

2

3

4

5

6

7

Cork Oak

Quercus suber

One of the most important economic plants of the Mediterranean, along with the olive and the vine, Cork Oak is easily recognized there by its bright brown trunk where the bark has been removed to give cork. Cork Oak is an untidy looking evergreen (**5**) sometimes growing 20m high, though more commonly half that. It is mainly grown in Portugal and southern Spain but is planted as far north as southern England.

BARK Before stripping, which is done about every 20 years, Cork Oaks have thick, deeply fissured grey bark (**1**).

LEAVES Small, dark, oval, rather prickly-edged (**2**), with a characteristic zig-zag midrib.

FLOWERS Male catkins (**3**) are conspicuous in early spring.

FRUIT Egg-shaped acorns (**4**) sit in fringed cups and ripen the same year.

RELATED SPECIES:

Lucombe Oak *Q.* x *crenata* is the hybrid with Turkey Oak (p. 124) and is more often seen in England. It is only half evergreen, the leaves falling in spring.

Holly Oak *Q. coccifera* has short-stalked, hairless, prickly leaves (**6**) and is a common scrubby tree in the Mediterranean region.

1

Wych Elm

Ulmus glabra

The most easily recognized elm, Wych Elm (**6**) is distinguished by its large, short-stalked leaves, and the absence of sucker shoots. The trunk often forks near the ground. Wych Elm is a common woodland tree, particularly in the north and west, and has shown considerable resistance to Dutch Elm disease. Wych derives from an old word for supple, referring to the twigs (**2**).

BARK Smooth at first but later develops thick, straight ribs and turns grey (**3**).

LEAVES Vary greatly in shape but are large and very rough to the touch (**5**). As in all elms, the base of the leaf extends further down the stalk on one side than the other, but in Wych Elm the long side crosses over the short stalk and hides it.

FLOWERS Red (**4**), appearing in late February.

FRUIT Winged (**1**), with the seed set centrally, visible before the leaves are expanded.

RELATED SPECIES:

Dutch Elm *U. x hollandica* is thought to be a hybrid with *U. minor*. Once common, but heavily reduced by Dutch Elm disease, it has cracked bark, many suckers and spreading branches. Huntingdon Elm var. *vegeta* has straighter branches but both have longer-stalked, smoother leaves (**7**) than Wych Elm, and seeds not in the middle of the fruit.

English Elm

Ulmus procera

English Elm was, before the advent of Dutch Elm disease, the classic hedgerow tree of the English lowlands, suckering vigorously to produce long lines of characteristic compact crowns (**6**). A variable tree with distinct local types maintained by vegetative propagation (suckering). Probably native, and now mainly found as a hedgerow shrub.

BARK Dark, finely ridged (**3**); twigs slim, hairy (**2**).

LEAVES English Elm is best distinguished by its small, rounded, rough-surfaced, dark green leaves (**5**), which are longer on one side at the base, but rounded where they join the stalk.

FLOWERS Red (**4**), produced in February or March, ripening by May, after the leaves have expanded.

FRUIT Ripe flowers give fruits (**1**) with the seed nearer the top of the round wing.

RELATED SPECIES:

Small-leaved Elm *U. minor* typically has narrower leaves (**7**), with the unequal base joining the stalk at right-angles, and oval fruit-wings. It is an exceptionally variable tree. reproducing by suckers to give distinctive local types such as Cornish, Wheatley, and Plot Elms (see pp. 136–7). Common in Europe, and probably introduced in Britain, it is now much reduced by disease.

Fluttering Elm *U. laevis* is a widespread tree of continental Europe with very long-stalked flowers (**8**).

ELMS: summer outlines

English, 134

Plot, 134

Small-leaved, 134

Wheatley, 134

NB: all to scale except English which is drawn smaller

Cornish, 134

Huntingdon, 132

Dutch, 132

Wych, 132

Southern Nettle Tree

Celtis australis

An elegant tree or shrub, whose rather regular crown (**6**) is usually borne on a long, straight trunk, Southern Nettle Tree has slender, curving branches and twigs (**1**). Widespread in southern Europe, south of the Alps, and west to France, in dry, rocky fields and by streams, often in scrub with plants such as Downy Oak (p. 126) and Flowering Ash (p. 222). Occasionally planted further north.

BARK Smooth, grey (**2**).

LEAVES Distinctive, toothed narrow oval (**4**), drawn out into a long curved point and softly hairy on the underside.

FLOWERS Appear in March–May (**3**), have tiny reddish-brown petals and large, conspicuous styles, but in addition to the normal hermaphrodite flowers with both stamens and styles, each tree bears male flowers as well.

FRUIT Small fleshy berries (**5**), about 1 cm across, on long flexuous stalks; the young fruits are off-white, ripening through dull red to a dull brownish violet.

1

2

hermaphrodite flower

Black Mulberry

Morus nigra

A short, unimpressive tree (**5**) rarely reaching
10m, Black Mulberry nevertheless often has a
disproportionately massive trunk. Black Mulberry
is a native of central Asia, widely planted for its
fruits as far north as southern England.
BARK Bright reddish-brown, extensively fissured
(**2**), and often massive protruding bosses.
LEAVES Large, oval (**3**), up to 20cm long, with
toothed margins some times deepening into lobes,
and fat, slightly hairy twigs (**1**).
FLOWERS Males and female flowers are separate
but on the same tree and have all their parts in
fours; they open in May.
FRUIT Unmistakable (**4**); resemble firm, juicy
raspberries, ripening from green to vermilion to a
deep dark purple in late summer and then sweet
and edible.
RELATED SPECIES:
White Mulberry *M. alba* is a slightly taller and
more elegant tree with slender branches and
hairless leaves (**6**) and twigs. Its fruits (**7**) vary from
whitish to purple and are stalked. A Chinese
species once cultivated as the food plant for
silkworms in southern Europe, but now less often
seen than Black Mulberry.

1

2

3

4

5

6

7

Fig

Ficus carica

The fig is an unmistakable tree with its large leaves and its rather lumpy appearance (**6**). The Fig is widely cultivated and naturalized in southern Europe, and planted in sheltered spots as far north as southern Scotland.

BARK Smooth, shiny, pale grey, on a short trunk which usually branches quite close to the ground. Twigs are stubby and ridged (**2, 5**) with a large green terminal bud.

LEAVES Large (20cm long), prominently but shallowly lobed, slightly greyish-green (**3**).

FLOWERS Separate male and female flowers are concealed in the fleshy, green fig itself (**4**).

FRUIT In the Mediterranean pollination is achieved by a minute gall-wasp which lays its eggs in some of the female flowers which have short styles and, in so doing, pollinates other flowers with longer styles; these mature and the fig begins to ripen, turning from green to purple-brown in the second year and swelling to 5–8cm (**1**).

variation in lobing

Tulip Tree

Liriodendron tulipifera

This fine tree is important in forests in the eastern United States. It forms a tall narrow crown (**5**) with branches curving downwards and then sharply up, supported by a massive trunk. Planted and common in parks to quite far north in Scotland.

BARK With grey, cracked bark coating the massive trunk (**2**). The twigs (**1**) bear long reddish, often curved buds.

LEAVES Unmistakable, lobed (**4**), ending in V-shaped notch, rather than a point.

FLOWERS Large (**3**), about 6cm across, produced in June, and have broad, curving, cup-like, green and orange petals, surrounding the rings of thick, fleshy, yellowish stamens.

FRUIT The fat green 'cone' in the centre of the flower ripens to produce a cluster of winged, brown fruits, which remain on the tree for some months.

RELATED SPECIES:
Magnolias are closely related trees, usually with simple pointed oval leaves (**7**). Some also have greenish flowers, but those most often planted have huge white or pink flowers, 10–15cm across (**6**). Commonest is *Magnolia* x *soulangeana*, but *M. stellata* with narrow petals, and the evergreen *M. grandiflora*, usually trained against a wall, are also not infrequently seen.

1

2

London Plane

Platanus x *hispanica*

London Plane is one of the few trees that can be identified with ease from its bark alone. It forms a tall stately tree (**6**) but is often also seen pollarded and cut back.

BARK Greyish-brown, flaking off to leave large yellowish patches (**2**).

LEAVES Pure green (**4**), with five well-marked pointed lobes each itself lined with large teeth; they appear late, usually towards the end of May. Its large rufous buds (**1**) have a small peg (the old leaf-scar) at their bases.

FLOWERS Female deep purplish-red (**3**), borne in small round balls on long stalks at the same time as the leaves.

FRUIT Female flowers mature to give the familiar, rough football-like plane fruits (**5**). The seeds are rarely viable, however, for London Plane is a hybrid between two trees, the Oriental Plane *P. orientalis* of Asia and south-east Europe, and the American Plane *P. occidentalis*. Where and when the hybrid appeared is a matter of controversy but it has proved without equal in withstanding the vicissitudes of city life – air pollution, poor soils etc – and has become one of the most familiar of urban trees.

1

2

3

4

5

6

Common Pear

Pyrus communis

A straggling tree (**6**), usually 10–15m high. In winter
the stubby 'short shoots' give the whole tree a
bristly appearance. Now a widely distributed but
never common hedgerow tree, from northern
England southwards.

BARK Dark, scaly, fissured (**2**); twigs rather
yellowish (**1**).

LEAVES Rounded, oval (**4**). Glossy, woolly beneath
when young, but finally hairless, and borne on long
stalks.

FLOWERS Common Pear flowers earlier than the
superficially similar Crab Apple (p. 152), nearly
always in April, sometimes by late March, when the
leaves are just emerging; flowers (**3**) are large, up to
4cm across, in loose, flat-topped heads, and have
conspicuous purple anthers.

FRUIT Common Pear is the parent of all cultivated
pears although sometimes wild specimens are
distinguished as Wild Pear *P. pyraster*. It has small,
hard, often rounded fruits (**5**), less than 4cm long
which can litter the ground below; cultivated varieties
can have fruits up to 15cm long, ripening soft.

RELATED SPECIES:

Wild Pear *P. cordata* is a thorny shrub found in
western France and near Plymouth and Truro. It has
a pointed flowerhead, smaller flowers, and a round,
finally red fruit, less than 2cm (**7**).

Willow-leaved Pear *P. salicifolia* is often planted.
Normally weeping, it has narrow, greyish leaves (**8**).

3

4

5

6

7

8

FLESHY FRUITS

Strawberry Tree, 220

Elder, 230

Alder Buckthorn, 208

Hawthorn, 164

Fig, 142

Medlar, 162

Nettle Tree, 138

Juniper, 40

Holly, 200

Snowy
Mespil, 160

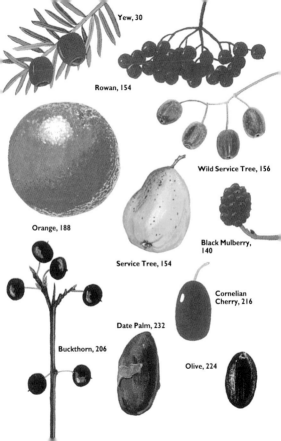

Yew, 30

Rowan, 154

Wild Service Tree, 156

Orange, 188

Service Tree, 154

Black Mulberry, 140

Cornelian Cherry, 216

Buckthorn, 206

Date Palm, 232

Olive, 224

Crab Apple

Malus sylvestris

Crab Apple is an often shrubby tree (**6**) common in hedges and woodland edges, but also occurring as a true woodland tree, mainly in oakwoods.

BARK Scaly bark (**2**) is often paler and smoother than that of Common Pear (p. 148)

LEAVES Rounded or oval leaves (**4**) which open woolly, but expand hairless, all borne on the stubby short shoots or spurs (**1**).

FLOWERS The large flat, white or pink 5-petalled flowers (**3**) can be up to 6cm across, in small flattened clusters, and appear after the leaves in May.

FRUIT The small fruits (**5**), about 2cm across, yellow when ripe, and sour, are borne on hairless stalks. Crab Apple occurs throughout Europe, north to southern Scotland.

RELATED SPECIES:

Cultivated Apple *M. domestica* occurs in so many varieties that a single description is impossible, but all have leaves (**7**) that remain woolly on the underside, and hairy stalks to the large, sweeter fruits (**8**) which may be red, green or yellow.

Rowan

Sorbus aucuparia

Rowan is an elegant, slender tree (**6**), reaching 15m or rarely more, and with steeply ascending branches. An important native tree of the whole European continent, but particularly common in the north and in mountain regions, and there reaching higher than other deciduous trees. Usually on infertile soils, often in areas of high rainfall, and common in upland moors and rocky slopes. Widely planted for its supposedly beneficial effect in driving away witches.

BARK Smooth, shining, grey-brown (**2**) until quite old.
LEAVES Distinctive, pinnate (**4**), typically with 6–7 pairs of leaflets. Young twigs (**1**) are slightly hairy, and the buds extremely so when bursting.
FLOWERS Attractive, creamy (**3**), produced in May, each less than 1cm across, but in dense flat-topped heads, 10–15cm across, usually stiffly erect and conspicuous.
FRUIT Almost spherical, 6–9mm, bright scarlet in August (**5**).
RELATED SPECIES:
True Service Tree *S. domestica* is a more massive tree with spreading branches, best distinguished by rough, scaly bark, larger flowers and larger, yellow-brown pear shaped fruits (**7**). Native on seacliffs in Glamorgan; widespread in southern Europe and occasionally planted further north.

Wild Service Tree

Sorbus torminalis

This unusual looking tree is often a puzzle when first seen, with its combination of deeply lobed leaves, somewhat resembling those of Plane (p. 146), white flowers, and small brown fruit. It has a neat crown and can reach 25m. A very widely distributed European tree, north to central England, but typically found as isolated individuals, often in clearings in woods on damp, rather infertile soils. In Britain, usually associated with English Oak (p. 118) and on the continent often with Downy Oak (p. 126).

BARK Flaking and lightly fissured (**2**).

LEAVES Glossy green (**4**), up to 10cm long, with 2–5 pairs of long-pointed toothed lobes, the whole leaf roughly triangular in shape. Its buds (**1**) are rounded and a striking clear green.

FLOWERS White (**3**), larger than those of Rowan (p. 154) and in more open clusters; appear in May and June.

FRUIT (**5**) Ripens in September, bright brown, oblong and rough-marked.

1

2

3

4

5

Whitebeam

Sorbus aria

In the open, Whitebeam produces a regular crown
(**8**) up to 20m high, but in woods it forms a mass of
steeply rising branches. Typical of woods and scrub
on chalk and limestone in western Europe, north to
central England; related species occur in Scotland
and Scandinavia.

BARK Smooth, grey-brown (**4**) until quite old and
buds (**3**) are long.

LEAVES Distinctive (**7**), usually oval, dull green
above with thick white hairs beneath so that in wind
the whole tree seems pale grey. The leaf margins are
toothed, not lobed. Leaf characters distinguish a large
number of closely-related species, mostly very rare.

FLOWERS Small, white (**5**), about 15mm across,
appear in loose, domed clusters in May and June.

FRUIT Scarlet, spherical or oblong fruits (**6**) appear
by September.

RELATED SPECIES:

Swedish Whitebeam *S. intermedia* is a native of
Scandinavia but is widely planted and often
naturalized. It has deeply lobed leaves (**9**), grey (not
white) beneath and larger fruits (**1**). Again many
rare allied species occur.

Broad-leaved Whitebeam *S. latifolia* is another
aggregate of similar species, including the hybrid of
Whitebeam and Wild Service Tree (p. 156), with
shallow leaf-lobes (**10**) and orange-brown fruits (**2**).
It resembles some of the rare native whitebeams.

Snowy Mespil

Amelanchier lamarckii

A startlingly beautiful tree when in flower, Snowy Mespil is perhaps most often seen as a straggling shrub (**5**) but occasionally reaches 10–12m. It usually forms a dense tangle of long shoots, branching from close to the ground, and lacking thorns but with narrow, pointed buds (**1**). A North American plant of doubtful origin, widely grown in parks and gardens, and sometimes naturalized, for example in Surrey.

BARK Smooth, dark (**2**).

LEAVES 5–6cm long, oval, but pointed, and edged with fine, even teeth (**4**). When first expanding in April they are strongly purplish and form a striking background to the mass of white flowers.

FLOWERS Have long narrow petals (**3**) up to 2cm, and are borne on long spikes, rising away from the branches.

FRUIT Small, spherical (**6**), 5–6cm in diameter, ripen through red to a deep, dark purple.

RELATED SPECIES:

The shrubby *A. ovalis* grows in rocky places in central Europe; it has more coarsely toothed leaves. *A. grandiflora*, another North American species, often grown in gardens and occasionally naturalized, has larger, shorter stalked fruits.

1

2

3

4

5

6

Medlar

Mespilus germanica

A curious looking, usually spiky shrub which, when cultivated, can be a small tree 5–6m high. Native in south-eastern Europe but cultivated since medieval times in western Europe and occasionally naturalized, most often in hedges.

BARK Greyish, flaking (**1**), revealing more brightly-coloured patches.
LEAVES Narrow (**3**), 10–15cm long, are a dull, almost olive-green above, and wrinkled and leathery; hairy below, and very short-stalked.
FLOWERS Large, white (**2**), 4–6cm across, appear singly in May, and the narrow, pointed sepals protrude between the petals.
FRUIT Hard, greenish, brown (**4**), spherical at the base but flat-topped and crowned by the sepals.

winter silhouette

1

2

3

4

Hawthorn

Crataegus monogyna

One of the most familiar sights of lowland Europe, Hawthorn is typically seen as a dense thorny shrub, but will readily form a small tree (**9**) up to 12m high. Common on all soils except the most acid, and the commonest hedge plant except in towns, where it has been supplanted by the monotony of Privet and Leyland Cypress.

BARK Bright brown, flaking (**5**).

LEAVES Variable but lobed (**7**) at least half-way to the midrib, normally with 3–4 pairs of lobes.

FLOWERS Appear in dense clusters (**6**) in late May and early June, each 10–15mm across, white, but turning pink as they mature; occasional pink or double-flowered forms occur and are much planted. Each flower has only one style (**1**) and one ovary (**3**) (hence *monogyna*).

FRUIT Familiar haws (**8**), deep red, sometimes purplish, ripe in September, but persisting on the trees if not stripped by birds.

RELATED SPECIES:

Midland Hawthorn *C. laevigata* is more of a woodland plant (**13**) and has leaves (**11**) lobed less than half-way to the midrib and flowers (**10**) with two styles (**2**) and ovaries (**4**). In Britain it is found mainly in the south-east growing with *C. monogyna* and hybridizing freely, but flowering a week or so earlier. Fruits (**12**) are also illustrated.

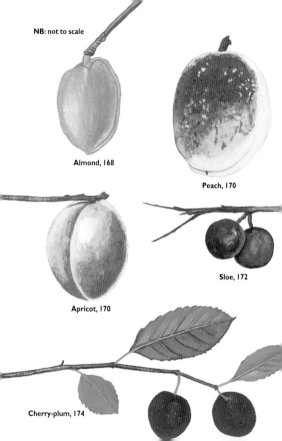

NB: not to scale

Almond, 168

Peach, 170

Apricot, 170

Sloe, 172

Cherry-plum, 174

CHERRIES AND PLUMS

Plum, 174

Damson, 174

Greengage, 174

Wild Cherry, 176

Cherry Laurel, 180

Bird Cherry, 178

St Lucie's Cherry, 178

Almond

Prunus dulcis

One of the many fruit trees whose cultivation is so ancient that the native range is unknown, Almond is unusual amongst its relatives in being grown for its nut rather than the fleshy fruit. Most often seen as a small tree (**6**), 5–10m high. Probably native to western Asia, but commonly planted, both for ornament in northern Europe, and also for the nut crop in the south.

BARK Very dark (**3**); wild trees, in southern Europe, have spiny twigs.

LEAVES Narrow (**5**), 7–12cm long, and spear-shaped, with a finely toothed margin; typically folded along the midrib.

FLOWERS One of the earliest suburban trees to flower, in March, its strong pink flowers (**4**) are 3–5cm across and conspicuous on the leafless branches.

FRUIT The well-known nut (**1**) is concealed in a flattened green fruit (**7**) and may persist so on the tree during winter. A winter twig (**2**) is also illustrated.

spiny twig

4

5

6

7

Apricot

Prunus armeniaca

This small tree is seen as an orchard crop in southern
Europe but further north most often trained against a
south facing wall. Apricot is probably a native of Asia.

LEAVES Long-stalked, oval (**4**), with very finely
toothed margins.

FLOWERS Delicate, pink (**3**), appear on the bare twigs
in March and April, often clustering at the tips of the
twigs. A winter twig (**1**) is also illustrated.

FRUIT Striking 'apricot'-coloured (**5**), fleshy and
rounded, with a well-marked notch, and a soft heavy
coat; ripens early – in June in the Mediterranean.

RELATED SPECIES:

Peach *P. persica* is slightly more hardy and can be
found in cultivation further north and in sheltered
corners north to Scotland. It has long narrow leaves
(**6**), resembling Almond, p. 168, but broadest above the
middle, and thin flexible twigs (**2**). The flowers (**7**) are a
deeper pink than Apricot and appear slightly later as
the leaves unfold: it has a very familiar and distinctive
fruit (**8**). larger than an Apricot and pinker. Probably a
native of China. A winter twig (**2**) is also illustrated.

Other *Prunus* species are planted for their fruits such
as Nectarine, whose fruit resembles a small, glossy
peach, or for ornament, including a very wide range of
Japanese cherries.

1

2

Blackthorn

Prunus spinosa

Blackthorn rarely forms a tree and is typically seen as an occasional plant in a hawthorn hedge, or as a densely tangled thicket (**5**); up to 4m tall, it is by far the commonest and most widespread European *Prunus*. Quickly recognized by its very dark thorny shoots (**1**) (hence 'Blackthorn'), which contrast strongly with the dense clusters of small white flowers which appear before the leaves, usually in late March or early April. Blackthorn is a native plant found throughout Britain in scrub, hedges and woodland edges, and occasionally persisting inside woods in shade. It will grow on almost any soil except for that of wet, acid peat-bogs.

LEAVES Small (2–4cm), narrow, oval and finely toothed (**3**).

FLOWERS Individual flowers (**2**) are 12–15mm across, clustered on the short shoots, and with conspicuous red anthers.

FRUIT The familiar sloe (**4**), firm rounded blue-black plums, about 1cm across, with an attractive purplish bloom and very bitter flesh; they are conspicuous from late August to October.

Cherry-plum or Myrobalan Plum

Prunus cerasifera

A shrub or small tree usually less than 10m high (**6**), Cherry-plum stands out in March as the first white-flowered blossom tree, flowering several weeks before Blackthorn, and at the same time as the young leaves (**2**). A native of south-eastern Europe but widely planted and usually found near houses, often in a purple-leaved form (var. *atropurpurea*).

BARK Rough-barked (**1**)

LEAVES Pointed, oval (**4**), up to 7cm long, borne on shiny, sometimes spiny twigs which stay green until their third year.

FLOWERS Resemble those of Blackthorn but occur in sparser groups and are larger, about 2cm across (**3**).

FRUIT Rather pinkish red, cherry-like (**5**); only mature in a hot summer in Britain.

RELATED SPECIES:

Wild Plum *P. domestica* probably derives from a hybrid of Cherry-plum and Blackthorn. It has grey-brown twigs and flowers later, in April and May. One type, Bullace, ssp. *instititia*, has downy twigs, small purple-black fruits, is often naturalized, and is probably the parent of the cultivated Damson. The Garden Plum, ssp. *domestica*, has greenish-white flowers and larger fruits of various colours: green (greengage (**8**)), purple (Czar), reddish-orange (Victoria (**7**)), etc.

Wild Cherry or Gean

Prunus avium

Wild cherry is much the most impressive tree amongst all its relatives, regularly reaching 20m or more. Open-grown trees have neat conical crowns (**7**). Wild Cherry grows throughout Europe. It is characteristic of wood-edges but can grow in full canopy, often in beechwoods.

BARK Purple-grey, shiny, peeling, horizontally-banded (**2**), coating the regular cylindrical trunk, often buttressed at the base.

LEAVES Buds are large, pointed and conspicuously russet against the grey twigs (**1**) and burst in April unfolding leaves that are initially bronze (**6**) and soon turn green. The leaves (**5**) typically hang limply and have two prominent knobs where they join the stalk.

FLOWERS Large, long-stalked, cup-shaped flowers (**3**) open in small clusters in April before or at the same time as the leaves. Double-flowered forms are often planted.

FRUIT A familiar cherry (**4**), ripening through yellow and bright red to dark purplish-red, but much favoured by birds.

RELATED SPECIES:
Sour Cherry *P. cerasus* is a shrubby plant with smaller, darker, short-stalked leaves (**8**) and rounded petals. Much cultivated – its varieties comprise most of the edible cherries (**9**) – it is widely but sparsely naturalised.

1

2

3

4

5

6

7

8

9

Bird Cherry

Prunus padus

Bird Cherry forms a small bushy tree (**6**) up to 15m
high, and frequently leafy almost to the ground. This
is the commonest cherry in Scotland and the upland
parts of northern England, and occurs through much
of Europe, south to the Alps. It grows in open, rocky
woods, by streams and in limestone pavements.

BARK Smooth, dark, aromatic (**2**) with prominent
orange flecks and brown twigs (**1**).

LEAVES Usually smaller than in Wild Cherry and
are dark green and leathery, with conspicuous
reddish petioles (**4**).

FLOWERS Bird Cherry is best recognized by having
its flowers (**3**) on long stiff spikes and not in clusters,
from 10–35 on each spike. Individual flowers appear
in May and are small, 10–15mm across, with slightly
ragged petals.

FRUIT Flowers mature to give shiny black cherries (**5**),
6–8mm across.

RELATED SPECIES:

St Lucie's Cherry *P. mahaleb* is shrubbier, with
small, rounded leaves, short spikes of only 3–10
flowers (**7**) and slightly larger fruits (**8**). It grows in
dry scrub in central Europe, extending to Belgium.

Black Cherry *P. serotina* is a North American tree,
often planted, which has dense spikes of smaller
flowers and purplish-black fruits.

1

2

3

4

5

6

7

8

Cherry Laurel

Prunus laurocerasus

Cherry Laurel is a widely planted and frequently naturalized shrub or small tree (**5**) that is regularly mistaken for a Rhododendron (p. 218). Though native only in south-east Europe, Cherry Laurel has been widely planted in western Europe and is often found as an understorey shrub, naturalized in woods in western Britain. The leaves produce cyanide when crushed.

BARK Dark grey (**1**) with small orange cracks.

LEAVES Long (up to 20cm), glossy, stiff, rather brittle (**3**), on short green stalks, less than 1cm long.

FLOWERS Appear in April and May, each 8–10mm across, on erect, 8–12cm long spikes (**2**).

FRUIT Flowers ripen to give shiny, purplish-black, oblong cherries (**4**) 10 by 15mm, in September.

RELATED SPECIES:

Portugal Laurel *P. lusitanica* is the other evergreen cherry that is sometimes planted in western Europe. It is a larger tree than Cherry Laurel, and its dark green leaves have red stalks up to 2.5cm long. Flowers (**6**) and fruit (**7**) are both smaller, usually failing to mature. It is a native in Spain and Portugal but rarely naturalized in Britain.

2

3

4

6

5

Laburnum

Laburnum anagyroides

A small tree (**6**) up to 8–10m high with green, hairy twigs (**1**), Laburnum is one of the most conspicuous features of the urban scene in late May and early June. The whole tree, but particularly the seeds, is extremely poisonous. Laburnum is native in southern and central Europe, mainly in open woods and scrub in hilly areas. Very widely planted in Britain, it is often found bird-sown far from houses.

BARK Smooth brownish-green (**2**).

LEAVES Compound (**4**), each with 3 leaflets, slightly hairy beneath.

FLOWERS Dramatic, densely borne on long hanging spikes (**3**) up to 25cm long, and sometimes almost covering the tree. Individual flowers are the characteristic pea-flower shape, about 2cm long.

FRUIT Dry, brown pods (**5**) open violently, throwing out the seeds.

RELATED SPECIES:

Scottish Laburnum *L. alpinum* has smaller flowers (**8**) in longer spikes, opening a few weeks later. Leaves (**7**) are larger and they and the twigs are hairless. Native in the Alps and surrounding area and planted mainly in Scotland. The hybrid between these, with long spikes of larger flowers and pods almost without seeds, is widely planted.

Judas Tree *Cercis siliquastrum* is a Mediterranean tree with heart-shaped leaves (**9**) and pink flowers.

1

2

Locust Tree

Robinia pseudoacacia

Locust Tree or False Acacia was one of the first North American trees to be introduced to this country where it thrives when planted in light soils, but only infrequently seeds itself. In southern Europe it is widely naturalized. It forms a massive tree (**7**), to 25m.

BARK Very rough, coarsely-ridged, shredding (**3**).

LEAVES Reddish twigs (**2**) bear pairs of spines and pinnate leaves (**6**) with 3–10 pairs of leaflets.

FLOWERS White (**5**) appear, in June in long (to 20cm) hanging spikes.

FRUIT Flattened pods (**1**) 5–10cm long.

RELATED SPECIES:

Pagoda or **Scholar's Tree** *Sophora japonica* is a superficially similar tree with no spines, narrower leaflets (**8**) and bark with broad, ridges. The creamy white flowers appear in upright spikes much later in the year. A Chinese tree, occasionally planted.

Honey-locust *Gleditsia triacanthos* is another North American tree usually recognized by the clusters of long, branched spines on its trunk (**4**), but spineless forms are planted. Male and female flowers are in separate spikes, ripening to give long twisted pendulous brown pods, which stay on the tree in the winter. Its leaves (**9**) are yellow-green. All have simply pinnate leaves in contrast to *Acacias* which have bipinnate leaves (**10**).

5

6

7

8

9

10

Mimosa

Acacia dealbata

Acacias are widely planted in the Mediterranean but are not hardy and so are seldom seen in Britain outside Devon and Cornwall. The best known is Mimosa, an extremely delicate small tree (**4**)

BARK Smooth, brown.

LEAVES Feathery (**1**), pinnate with pinnate leaflets. There may be up to 20 pairs of leaflets, each with up to 50 pairs of short leaflets only 3–4mm long, giving an ethereal appearance.

FLOWERS Pale yellow (**2**), are in small ball-like heads 5–6mm across, in long clusters, produced very early in the year.

FRUIT Flattened brown pods (**3**) up to 10cm long.

RELATED SPECIES:

Blackwood Acacia *A. melanoxylon* is a tree up to 40m tall which has similar leaves when young, but when mature has simple oblong leaves (**5**). The flower-heads are larger and white. Planted in south-west Europe.

Many other *Acacias* are planted in southern Europe and occasionally naturalized.

1

2

3

4

5

Citrus

The familiar citrus fruit include half a dozen or so types that are grown in Europe. All are closely related and several may be grafted onto a single stock. In addition to the familiar oranges, lemons, and grapefruit, the large-fruited citron *Citrus medica* and shaddock *C. grandis* are sometimes grown, the latter resembling an almost spineless grapefruit *C. paradisi*. The tangerine *C. deliciosa* is also sometimes found.

Sweet Orange *Citrus sinensis* is the most widely cultivated species, however, being planted in large groves in the Mediterranean region. It is a small evergreen tree (**4**) with weak spines.
LEAVES Pointed, leathery, dark (**2**) on winged stalks.
FLOWERS Appear in short spikes (**1**) in April and are white and strongly fragrant.
FRUIT The familiar fruits (**3**) are solid at the core.
RELATED SPECIES:
Seville Orange *C. aurantium* is the best marmalade orange, with acid juice and a hollow in the centre of the thick-rinded fruit (**5**). Leaves have broad wings to the stalk where it joins the leaf.
Lemon *C. limon* (**6**) has some flowers only male and stronger spines. Leaf-stalks hardly winged. Lemon has many more stamens than other Citrus species except for the very similar sweet lime *C. limetta*.

Tree of Heaven

Ailanthus altissima

A tall, elegant tree (**4**), frequently reaching 20m and occasionally more, it has a long, unbranched trunk. Tree of Heaven is a native of China, but it is widely planted, particularly in towns as it seems resistant to aerial pollution. and it is occasionally naturalized.

BARK Smooth, grey.

LEAVES Tree of Heaven is late into leaf, remaining bare until June and then unfolding large, pinnate ash-like leaves (**3**) each with 6–12 pairs of leaflets up to 12cm long, the whole leaf being as long as 60cm. The leaflets are toothed at the base and glossy and wrinkled on the top surface. The twigs (**1**) are fat and orange, and have prominent leaf-scars, somewhat reminiscent of Horse Chestnut (p. 198).

FLOWERS This species has both separate male and female flowers and normal hermaphrodite ones, and individual trees may be wholly male, wholly female, or somewhere in between. The flowers (**2**) open in July, each 7–8mm across, greenish-white, in long branching spikes on the ends of the shoots.

FRUIT Winged (**5**), each with a central seed, again rather similar to Ash (p. 222), but ripening to a bright reddish-brown in September.

1

Norway Maple

Acer platanoides

A widespread but often overlooked tree, Norway Maple suddenly becomes very conspicuous for a few weeks in early April when the striking golden-yellow flowers open, on bare brown twigs. It forms a fine tree up to 30m tall (**5**) with a short unbranched trunk. A native tree of Scandinavia and the European mountains. Norway Maple is often planted, sometimes in dark-leaved or variegated forms, and the typical form readily seeds itself.

BARK Grey, smooth or finely-ridged (**2**).

LEAVES Twigs (**1**) and leaves (**4**) are both hairless, the latter a bright pure green with 5 fine-pointed toothed lobes giving a delicate, somewhat spiky appearance.

FLOWERS Small (**3**) (8mm across), borne in upright clusters containing both male and female flowers, open before the leaves expand and before the flowers of the related Sycamore (p. 196).

FRUIT The typical winged maple fruits (samaras) are olive-coloured and occur in pairs (**6**), the wings making an angle of 150°.

1

2

Norway Maple

Sycamore

Field Maple

Acer campestre

A small, rather ungainly tree (**6**) usually 10–15m high, though rarely as much as 25m, Field Maple is also a common hedgerow shrub. Field Maple is a common tree of lowland England, in woods and old hedges, and extends south to the Mediterranean, though there rarely and in hilly areas.

BARK The trunk bears fissured, flaky, grey-brown bark (**2**), orange-brown when freshly exposed.

LEAVES The young twigs (**1**) are slightly hairy and the small (4–8cm) deep green leaves (**4**) have 5 (occasionally 3) rounded lobes, and are downy on the underside; in autumn they turn a deep golden-red.

FLOWERS Separate male and female flowers (**3**) are borne on each tree, both in sparse, upright clusters which appear in May after the leaves have opened.

FRUIT In pairs whose wings spread almost horizontally at an angle of nearly 180° (**5**).

RELATED SPECIES:

Montpellier Maple *A. monspessulanum* is usually smaller and has the wings of the pairs of fruits almost parallel (**8**), and sometimes reddish. Otherwise it resembles a Field Maple with darker, somewhat leathery, three-lobed leaves (**7**). It grows in dry scrub throughout the Mediterranean and north to West Germany, and is occasionally planted elsewhere.

1

2

3

4

5

6

7

8

Sycamore

Acer pseudoplatanus

Sycamore is by far the commonest maple in Britain. It forms a magnificent domed tree (**7**) up to 35m tall. A native tree of the central and northern European mountains, it is introduced in Britain where it has become an essential part of the British scene and is often the most vigorous tree in upland areas. Ecologically it somewhat resembles Ash (p. 222).

BARK Starts smooth and grey (**3**) but soon cracks and finally becomes flaking and rough. The twigs (**2**) are stout and bear fat, green buds.

LEAVES Large (up to 15cm), dark green (**6**), with 5 pointed toothed lobes, are almost invariably seen (except in towns) blotched by the fungus *Rhytisma acerinum* and often by crimson galls.

FLOWERS Hang in long spike-like clusters (**4**), up to 100 in each, appearing in April along with the leaves.

FRUIT In pairs (**5**) with wings at about 90°, and after falling germinate in vast numbers the following spring to give the familiar seedlings (**1**).

RELATED SPECIES:

Italian Maple *A. opalus* is a smaller Mediterranean tree, with wings of the fruit (**9**) making an angle of about 30° or less. It has larger flowers and smaller leaves (**8**) with shallower lobes.

4

5

6

7

8

9

Horse Chestnut

Aesculus hippocastanum

One of the most familiar trees in areas near houses, Horse Chestnut is not in fact a native of Britain, but was introduced from southeast Europe in the seventeenth century. It forms a billowing, spreading, dome (**6**) typically up to 25m high but occasionally as much as 35m on a massive trunk. The name chestnut derives from the resemblance to the true, edible Chestnut (p. 114); Horse Chestnuts are inedible but very hard, and possessed of qualities endearing them to children. Very commonly planted and often naturalised.

BARK Cracks off in long plates (**3**).

LEAVES Rich brown buds (**2**) are large, up to 3.5cm long, and sticky, bursting to unfold the unmistakable oval leaflets (**5**), up to 25cm long.

FLOWERS Most trees flower in May, though some are early into leaf (in March) and flower (in April), becoming covered with the tall upright candelabras (**1**) of white, unequally 5-petalled flowers (**7**), each crimson blotched in the centre.

FRUIT In late September the mature fruits (**4**) fall, their green spiny shells splitting to reveal 1–3 shiny brown nuts.

RELATED SPECIES:

Pink Horse Chestnut *A.* x *carnea* is smaller and often poorly grown, with pink flowers (**8**). It is often planted.

Holly

Ilex aquifolium

Holly is not a tree that can be readily confused with any other. Holly forms a shrub with leafy branches right down to ground level (since grazing animals understandably avoid it) or a tree (**5**) occasionally as high as 20m, and is completely evergreen. A native of western Europe, common in lowland areas, but occurring throughout Britain except for the far north, Holly is a typical hedgerow tree and may form an understorey in oak, and especially beech, woods. Often planted for ornament or shelter, sometimes as variegated varieties.

BARK Smooth, grey (**1**).

LEAVES Tough, shiny, dark green (**2**), with undulating margins, normally lobed and with the lobes ending in stiff, sharp spines. Upper leaves and, rarely, those of all or most of the tree may be spineless and almost smooth-edged (**4**), possibly leading to confusion with evergreen oaks, such as Holm Oak (p. 128).

FLOWERS Small, 7–8mm across (**3**), male and female on separate trees; they are white and fragrant in May but may occur during the summer.

FRUIT Round berries (**6**) are prominent, though green, as early as July, and redden in September to the familiar berry. In mild winters they may survive the depredations of thrushes and other birds through to March.

1

Spindle-tree

Euonymus europaeus

Though able to grow into a small tree up to about 6m tall,
Spindle-tree is most often found in scrub on calcareous
soil, often with privet. Widespread in Europe north of the
Mediterranean as far as southern Scotland and Sweden,
Spindle-tree is quite common on chalk and limestone in
lowland Britain. The name derives from the use of its
wood for spindles in the spinning of wool.

BARK The Spindle-tree rarely has a single trunk, but the
main stems have grey-green bark.

LEAVES Twigs (1) have four angles and are smooth and
hairless, bearing opposite pairs of narrow oval, pointed,
bright green leaves (2).

FLOWERS Small greenish-white flowers (3) appear in May,
with 4 narrow, widely-spaced petals, in clusters of 3–8.

FRUIT The extraordinary fruits (4) are conspicuous in
late September and October, the seeds being covered by a
bright orange fleshy structure (the 'aril') and enclosed in a
cherry-pink capsule: the combination is unmistakable.

RELATED SPECIES:
Broad-leaved Spindle-tree *E. latifolius* has longer and
much broader leaves (6), 4–12 flowered clusters of 5-
petalled flowers, and a larger fruit capsule (5) up to 2cm
across. Native in central Europe and frequently planted
elsewhere.

1

Box

Buxus sempervirens

Box is such a familiar garden hedging plant (**5**), the dwarf cultivar often being trimmed to within a few inches of the ground, that it comes as a surprise to find it forms a respectable small tree from 6–10m high, if left to itself. In tree form (**4**) it has one or a few slightly twisted trunks. As a native it occurs scattered throughout western Europe, and in Britain only in a few isolated localities on chalk in southern England, the best known of which is Box Hill in Surrey. It is also very commonly planted as a hedge or thicket, sometimes as pheasant cover.

BARK Brown, cracked.

LEAVES Glossy, dark evergreen (**1**), borne in opposite pairs on the square stems and usually have their edges rolled under.

FLOWERS Yellowish (**2**), easily missed in April, tucked away among the leaves; the clusters contain both male and female flowers, but neither has petals.

FRUIT Small, dry capsule (**3**), with three short prongs. Only matures in a good summer in Britain.

Box Hill

Buckthorn

Rhamnus catharticus

Buckthorn is a large bush, usually about 5m tall, which sometimes can grow into a small tree up to 10m high. Even then it usually has a well-branched trunk. Branches are produced in opposite pairs almost at right-angles to the main shoot (**2**), but some only develop as short shoots bearing leaves, or even as rather blunt spines. Buckthorn is a common shrub on a wide range of soils from dry chalk to fen peat, mainly in lowland England. It is found throughout Europe from the Alps to southern Scandinavia.

BARK Dark, rather orange-brown, scaly (**1**).

LEAVES Leaf buds have dark scales; the oval leaves (**3**) have long stalks and 2–4 pairs of spreading veins; in autumn they turn brownish-yellow, in contrast to the superficially similar Alder Buckthorn (p. 208).

FLOWERS Small, 4-petalled, 4–5mm across and yellowish-green, and are produced in inconspicuous groups well back from the tips of the branches in May; male (**5**) and female (**6**) are separate.

FRUIT Berries (**4**) are glossy black in late September and October; they are poisonous with a powerful purgative (hence *catharticus*) effect.

1

Alder Buckthorn

Frangula alnus

Alder Buckthorn is sometimes confused with Buckthorn (p. 206) but rarely grows larger than 4 or 5m and forms only a bushy small tree (**5**). It has no thorns and the branches are not quite opposite each other and make a narrow angle with the main stem. Alder Buckthorn occurs throughout Europe from the Mediterranean northwards, except for northern mountains and islands; it is not found at all in Scotland. In England it occurs widely but is absent from large areas. It prefers moist, peaty soils and tolerates more acid soils than Buckthorn.

BARK Smooth, finely-cracked (**1**).

LEAVES Leaf buds (**2**) have no scales; the yellowish-green leaves (**3**) have 7–8 pairs of veins and turn a bright yellow in autumn.

FLOWERS Tiny, greenish-white (**4**), even smaller (3–4mm) than those of Buckthorn, and appear in small clusters at the tips of the branches.

FRUIT Glossy black berries (**6**), which ripen slightly later than those of Buckthorn, maturing from green through a rich cherry-red.

1

Small-leaved Lime

Tilia cordata

A fine tree, reaching 25–30m with an uneven crown (**5**), billowing out irregularly. Limes are among the latest of trees to flower, usually in early July. Small-leaved Lime is found throughout most of Europe, but only scattered in Britain, mainly in the Midlands, where it forms woods on deep, loamy soils. It is frequently planted.

BARK Greyish, and finely cracked (**2**), but broken by prominent bosses; sometimes ridged; young twigs (**1**) are slightly downy but soon become smooth and hairless.

LEAVES Quite small (**4**), rarely more than 7cm long, and heart-shaped, narrowing to a pointed tip, glossy dark green above and greyish and hairless beneath, with small tufts of orange-brown hairs.

FLOWERS Characteristic and unmistakable flower clusters arise from a long leaf-like bract and are half-upright. Each cluster has 4–12 yellowish-white 5-petalled flowers (**3**).

FRUIT Smooth and rounded (**6**) with a short beak; falls from the tree in a cluster, with the bract acting as a wing.

Common Lime

Tilia x europaea

A magnificent, tall tree (**3**) commonly reaching 25m, and in some places exceeding 40m. It is a hybrid between Small-leaved (p. 210) and Large-leaved Limes (below). A well-established hybrid, it reproduces largely by suckers. It occurs naturally, though sparsely, throughout Europe, but is very commonly planted, particularly in avenues.

BARK Long ridges and cracks and sprouting bosses (**2**).

LEAVES Larger than in Small-leaved Lime (**5**), from 6–10cm long, with tufts of whitish hairs underneath. The twigs (**1**) are hairless.

FLOWERS In clusters (**4**) of 5–10 flowers that dangle from the twigs, opening in July.

FRUIT Ripe fruits are faintly ribbed (**6**).

RELATED SPECIES:

Large-leaved Lime *T. platyphyllos* usually has a clean, unbossed trunk and leaves (**7**) that are downy underneath and sometimes above as well. Flowers usually in threes, opening often in late June, always earlier than other limes; the fruit (**8**) is strongly ribbed. Widespread in central and southern Europe, and forming woods in steep limestone slopes in the Welsh Marches, around Bristol and in south Yorkshire, but possibly a long-established introduction; widely planted.

Blue Gum

Eucalyptus globulus

Gum trees are tall and very fast-growing
Australasian trees with evergreen foliage,
normally distinct on young and old branches.
They are very widely planted in the
Mediterranean for timber, shelter and amenity.
Blue Gum is scarcely hardy in England but
common in Ireland and further south. It is a large
tree (**7**) reaching 40m.

BARK Multicoloured, peeling (**2**), fading from
oranges and pinks when new to a greyish-brown.

LEAVES Unstalked on young shoots (**3**) and
blue-grey; those on the old shoots (**6**) are sickle-
shaped, greener and up to 30cm long.

FLOWERS Have a curious disc-like structure (**5**)
with a ring of stamens; they occur individually.

FRUIT Very large (**1** and **4**), up to 3cm.

RELATED SPECIES:
Cider Gum *E. gunnii* is one of the hardiest
species and by far the most commonly planted in
England and occasionally surviving in Scotland. It
has rounded, blue, unstalked juvenile leaves and
larger, narrower, pointed mature leaves (**8**). It
flowers in July. Though quite hardy it still
succumbs to severe frosts.

A dozen or so other *Eucalyptus* species are
grown in Europe but few are hardy in the north.

Cornelian Cherry

Cornus mas

A small tree, reaching 8–10m, or a spreading, much-branched shrub (**5**). Cornelian Cherry occurs throughout lowland central Europe in open woods and scrub, usually on chalk and limestone; it is widely planted in gardens, sometimes in a variegated form, and is occasionally naturalized in Britain.

BARK Smooth (**2**).

LEAVES Pointed, oval (**4**), with prominent veins, borne in pairs along the twigs.

FLOWERS Cornelian Cherry flowers very early, in February and March, producing conspicuous tight clusters of bright yellow flowers (**3**) on the bare greyish-green twigs (**1**). Individual flowers have four tiny pointed petals, 2–3mm long, and the whole cluster sits on four yellow-green bracts that soon fall.

FRUIT Unusual and lozenge-shaped (**6**), the fruits are a rich bright red and give this plant its inappropriate name; they are 12–15mm long.

detail of flowers

Rhododendron

Rhododendron ponticum

A massive spreading shrub or small tree (**4**), this is the rhododendron that is frequently encountered as an almost complete shrub layer, particularly in oak or birch woods on acid sandy or dry peaty soils. *R. ponticum* is native in south-west and south-east Europe but is so widely planted and so readily sets seed that it has become widely naturalized mainly as a hybrid with *R. maximum*.

BARK (**1**).

LEAVES Large many-scaled buds, and dark green leathery leaves (**2**), paler underneath and up to 25cm long.

FLOWERS In dense clusters at the tips of the branches, surrounded by a ruff of leaves. They appear in June and each has the shape of a spreading bell (**3**) and is a striking pinkish-purple, up to 6cm across, and with 10 stamens.

FRUIT The seeds are produced in a dry capsule.

RELATED SPECIES:

Yellow Rhododendron *R. luteum* is smaller and deciduous, its 5-stamened yellow flowers (**5**) appearing on the leafless shoots in April and May. A rare native of central and south-east Europe, it is often grown in gardens and is occasionally naturalized.

Many other tree-forming *Rhododendron* species are planted but none are naturalized.

1

2

3

4

5

Strawberry Tree

Arbutus unedo

In the wild, in south-west Ireland and in the Mediterranean, Strawberry Tree is normally a large spreading shrub up to 2–3m high, but in cultivation it reaches 10–12m (**4**). In the Mediterranean it grows in dry, rock scrublands, in Ireland on rocky islands in lakes, and in oak scrub. Also a common garden plant in southern England.

BARK Dark brown (**1**), peels off in strips, revealing fresh red-brown flashes.

LEAVES Narrow, glossy, dark green, hairless (**3**), up to 10cm long and 2–3 times as long as wide.

FLOWERS This species flowers very late in the year, from late September onwards, its creamy flask-shaped flowers (**2**) produced in hanging, red-stalked clusters of 15–20.

FRUIT Takes a whole year to mature, so that at the same time the plant bears small clusters (rarely more than half a dozen survive to fruition) of bright orange-red warty footballs (**5**), which, from some fanciful resemblance to strawberries, give the plant its name; there is, of course, no relationship, the true Strawberry belonging to the Rose Family, the Strawberry Tree to the Heather Family.

1

2

3

4

5

Ash

Fraxinus excelsior

The only native tree of the Olive Family, Ash forms a rather untidy, crown (**8**), often with prominent dead branches, 20–25m high – exceptionally 40m. The trunk is often long and straight. An important woodland tree, Ash forms pure stands on limestones and in upland areas. In northern England it is the main hedgerow tree. Widespread in Europe.

BARK Initially smooth and grey, becomes split by long ridges and fissures on older trees (**2**). The twigs (**5**) give ash-woods a grey glow in winter, and bear distinctive large black buds (**4**).

LEAVES Pinnate (**7**) with 3–7 pairs of leaflets each up to 10cm long. It is one of the last native trees to come into leaf, and the leaves usually fall when still green.

FLOWERS May be male (**6**), female or hermaphrodite, as may whole trees; they appear in April before the leaves and, if male, are dark purple.

FRUIT Shed in October (**1**), and each is set in a long narrow brown wing, notched at the tip - the samaras or 'keys'.

RELATED SPECIES:

Manna or flowering Ash *F. ornus* is a smaller tree with smooth bark (**3**), grey-brown buds, smaller leaves (**9**) and prominent white flowers (**10**). Native of the Mediterranean widely planted.

2

3

Olive

Olea europaea

A grove of olives is the quintessential Mediterranean view, immortalized by Van Gogh. Olive is in fact a native tree of the Mediterranean, and the cultivated variety has larger leaves and fruits. It is a squat tree (**6**) reaching 15m, with a massive, often contorted, trunk. Wild trees occur in scrub in dry rocky places, and groves of cultivated olives are found all over the Mediterranean.

BARK Grey, fissured (**1**).

LEAVES Cultivated plants have narrow greyish leaves (**2**) but the wild variety has rounded leaves and spiny twigs.

FLOWERS Produced in short spikes (**3**) arising from the base of the leaves, each very small, with four whitish petals.

FRUIT Flowers mature to give the familiar fruits (**4**) green at first and finally black (**5**), from which the economically important oil is pressed.

wild branch

1

Foxglove Tree

Paulownia tomentosa

Foxglove Tree derives its name more from its membership of the same botanical family as foxglove than from the rather forced similarity between their flowers. It is a medium-sized tree (**4**), usually 10–15m high, but occasionally more, with an open crown. A Chinese tree widely planted in southern Europe and less often north to southern England.

BARK Smooth, grey.

LEAVES (**2**, much reduced, and **3**) Heart-shaped with a long, tapering point, 30–35cm long, and downy on both sides. This gives them a dull green colour and combined with their tendency to hang limply from the branches lends the tree a somewhat weary appearance. Some leaves may be larger and lobed.

FLOWERS Large (5cm long) (**1**), violet-blue withe deep tubes and five spreading lobes. They appear in June before the leaves in tall irregular spikes.

FRUIT Pale green, oblong, tough, with a small, pointed beak (**5**), eventually splitting when brown to release the winged seeds.

seed capsule   seed (x2.5)

Indian Bean Tree

Catalpa bignonioides

The Indians referred to here are American, for this is an introduced species from the southern United States, and despite its frost-tenderness, much favoured for planting in southern England. In general appearance it resembles a greener version of Foxglove Tree (p. 226), but it comes into leaf very late – in late June – and has white flowers, giving it something of the appearance of a small Horse Chestnut (**6**).

BARK Ridged, scaly (**2**), fat twigs with prominent leaf scars (**1**).

LEAVES Have a rounded base or slightly heart-shaped (**4**).

FLOWERS Both flower spike and flowers (**5**) are similar in shape to Foxglove Tree, but are white, and open in July.

FRUIT The extraordinary seed pods (**3**) are perhaps its most distinctive feature of this species, and give the plant its name. They are up to 40cm long and hang from the branches through the winter. Commonly planted in southern Europe and occasionally naturalized.

1

2

seed

3

4

5

6

Elder

Sambucus nigra

A familiar shrub or small tree (**7**), reaching 10m exceptionally, Elder behaves more like a weed than a tree, springing up with astonishing speed on disturbed ground and in cracks in concrete paths and similar places. Common throughout Europe except the far north, usually on disturbed soils and, since its leaves are unpleasant-tasting, it grows well around rabbit burrows.

BARK On mature trunks bark (**3**) is brown and deeply furrowed, on younger branches it is smooth with well-marked pores (lenticels) (**1**). If a twig is broken the wood is very soft and pithy (**2**).

LEAVES Pinnate (**6**), usually with 2–3 pairs of leaflets which vary from rounded to narrow oval, and occasionally may be deeply toothed.

FLOWERS Minute, about 5mm across, but are prominent in profuse, flat-topped clusters (**4**), 10–20cm across, appearing in June and smelling of cats. The flower clusters stand upright in flower but bend down with the weight of the fruit.

FRUIT Ripen in late August and September (**5**), the familiar black elderberries, edible and striking on their red stalks.

RELATED SPECIES:
Red-berried Elder *S. racemosa* has a rounded flowerhead and red berries (**8**). Central Europe and Scandinavia; naturalized in northern England and especially in Scotland.

1

2

3

Date Palm

Phoenix dactylifera

Palms are quite unmistakable: being monocotyledons (like grasses, sedges and lilies) their stems are not woody but fibrous and continually grow giving a cluster of leaves perched as much as 20m from the ground (**2**). In spite of the fact that Date Palms need a true hot desert climate in order for the fruit to ripen, the tree is widely planted for ornament throughout the Mediterranean.

BARK The trunk is largely made up of the old leaf bases which remain in a series of conspicuous spirals on the trunk (**1**).

LEAVES Huge, several metres long, with many pairs of long, narrow, greyish leaflets.

FLOWERS Borne in massive dangling clusters (**3**) arising from the top of the trunk.

FRUIT Immature green fruits (**4**) are all that is usually seen in Europe; to ripen into the familiar date (**5**) they need a true hot desert climate.

RELATED SPECIES:

Canary Palm *P. canariensis* is a smaller tree (**6**) up to 10m, with a fat trunk, bright green leaves and dry fruits. A native of the Canaries, it is often planted in the Mediterranean.

leaf

1

236

Index of Scientific Names